# Courage and Compassion

## TEN CANADIANS WHO MADE A DIFFERENCE

### Rona Arato

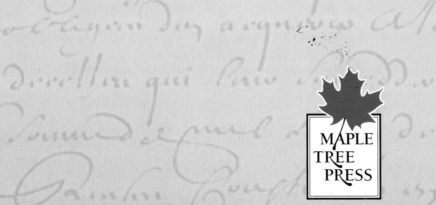

MAPLE TREE PRESS

**Maple Tree Press books are published by Owlkids Books Inc.**
10 Lower Spadina Avenue, Suite 400, Toronto, Ontario  M5V 2Z2
www.mapletreepress.com

Distributed in Canada by Raincoast Books
9050 Shaughnessy Street, Vancouver, British Columbia V6P 6E5

Distributed in the United States by Publishers Group West
1700 Fourth Street, Berkeley, California 94710

**Dedication**
For Paul

**Acknowledgments**
I want to thank the people who generously helped with this book. Steven
Cook and Barbara Carter of the Uncle Tom's Cabin Historic Site in Dresden,
Ontario, provided information and photos for the Josiah Henson chapter.
Judy Feld Carr shared her story, as did Elijah Harper. The Save the Children
Foundation, the Ladybug Foundation, and June Callwood's family allowed us
to use their photos. To Sheba Meland and Anne Shone of Maple Tree Press, a
special thank you for bringing these stories to life. Thanks to Paul for insisting
that I make this book the best it can be. And to the Writing Group, Anne,
Lynn, Frieda, and Sydell, who read, reread, critiqued, and encouraged me all
along the way: may we continue to go from strength to strength.

**Cataloguing in Publication Data**
Arato, Rona
     Courage and compassion : ten Canadians who made
a difference / Rona Arato.

(Wow Canada! book)
Includes index.
ISBN 978-1-897349-34-2 (bound).      ISBN 978-1-897349-35-9 (pbk.)

1. Canada — Biography — Juvenile literature. 2. Heroes — Canada —
   Biography — Juvenile literature.  I. Title.  II. Series.

FC25.A75 2008          j971.009'9          C2008-902044-8

**Library of Congress Control Number** 2008925719

**Design:** Céleste Gagnon

We acknowledge the financial support of the Canada Council for the Arts, the   **ONTARIO ARTS COUNCIL** / **CONSEIL DES ARTS DE L'ONTARIO**
Ontario Arts Council, the Government of Canada through the Book Publishing
Industry Development Program (BPIDP), and the Government of Ontario through
the Ontario Media Development Corporation's Book Initiative for our publishing
activities.

Printed in China

A    B    C    D    E    F

# Contents

# What Is a Hero?

Heroes are people who stand up for their beliefs. There are many kinds of heroes. A hero challenges a bully, protects a friend, or helps those who are hurt by war, famine, or disease. Firefighters, soldiers, and health care workers who risk their health, or even their lives, to help others are heroes. People who fight for human rights are heroes. You'll meet ten of them in this book.

## What Are Human Rights?

Human rights are the basic liberties that all human beings are entitled to, such as the right to food and clean drinking water; fair courts of law; the freedom to speak, worship, read books, and live wherever they want. Often, however, people are denied their human rights because of their nationality, religion, gender, or politics.

Imagine if you weren't allowed to go to school or to live in a certain neighbourhood because of the colour of your skin or your religion. What if someone *owned* you? Slaves, such as those in the southern United States before 1864, were considered property that could be bought and sold like cattle. There are parts of the world today where slavery still exists. In some countries children are forced to work long hours in factories, without being paid, educated, or even properly fed.

At times, governments abolish rights that are already part of a country's laws, as the Nazi government in Germany did for Jewish people during the Second World War. The Nazis even abolished their ultimate freedom—the right to exist—by killing 6 million Jewish people. This is known as the Holocaust.

Following the horrors of the Second World War, the **United Nations (UN)** was formed to ensure that human rights abuses, such as the Holocaust, would never happen again. On December 10, 1948, the UN adopted the **"Universal Declaration of Human Rights."** The declaration's purpose is to guarantee that people everywhere can expect certain basic freedoms: the right to life; liberty; personal security; an adequate standard of living; education; property; freedom of speech, thought, conscience, and religion; asylum from persecution; and freedom from torture. But some countries have chosen to ignore the declaration and in many parts of the world, people continue to suffer persecution, slavery, and a lack of civil liberties.

There are organizations at work to correct these wrongs. Alongside these organizations stand committed individuals, like those who are profiled in this book, whose work fuels their efforts. The heroes in this book are people who have fought for human rights because of their belief that everyone is entitled to freedom, justice, and good living conditions.

Jeanne Mance gave up the comfortable life of nobility in France to found the new settlement of Montréal and to nurse the people who lived there. Josiah Henson heroically helped slaves flee from the southern United States to freedom in Canada. Nellie McClung endured personal attacks and ridicule to ensure that Canadian women were legally recognized as persons, with the same rights and privileges as men. Roger Obata fought for an apology and compensation for the Japanese Canadians who were forced from their homes during the Second World War. Craig Kielburger has worked to end child labour around the world, giving up his free time, pocket money, and holidays to speak for children who cannot speak for themselves. And Hannah Taylor was only five years old when she started collecting money to help homeless people.

Each of the people you'll meet in this book shows us that by standing up for what you believe, a person can, and often does, make a significant difference in the lives of others. These heroes are all Canadian. Because of people like them, Canada is known as a country that fights for human rights around the world. And you, too, can be a hero. Next time you see someone bullied or discriminated against because of skin colour, religion, or a disability, stick up for that person. Standing up for what you believe in will show the right way to those around you, and will make you feel good, too.

# Jeanne Mance
## The Angel of the Colony

Jeanne looked down at the row of men stretched out on the ground inside the small hospital tent. They had been attacked by Iroquois. Jeanne had seen war injuries in France, both as a young girl and as a nurse. But this time she was in charge. This was her hospital and these were her patients. Gathering her courage, Jeanne began issuing orders to her helpers—bring water, bandages, ointments—even as she pushed away the fear coiled in the pit of her stomach. The Iroquois had attacked once; they would attack again. How long could the tiny settlement of Ville-Marie hold out? How long could she?

Even wealth could not shield Jeanne Mance from the horrors of the world she lived in. During her youth a series of wars and plagues killed hundreds of people in the town of Langres in the Champagne region of France where she was born. Europe was engulfed in the Thirty Years War, which was actually a series of wars that were fought all over Europe from 1618 to 1648. When Jeanne was in her late teens, she wanted to help the people she saw suffering. In those days there were no nursing schools. Jeanne got her training by volunteering to nurse wounded soldiers.

In the early 17th century, very little was known about hygiene and medicine, but Jeanne knew that she wanted to help others.

Jeanne was born on November 12, 1606, into a noble family. Her father, Charles Mance, was the *procureur du roi* (the king's attorney). When Jeanne was twenty, her mother, Catherine, died, and Jeanne helped raise her ten brothers and sisters. Jeanne was thirty-three years old when her father died. By this time her siblings were grown and had lives of their own. Suddenly Jeanne was alone and unmarried, not typical for a woman of her time. Most single women her age entered religious orders and became nuns. Although Jeanne was a deeply spiritual person, she did not want to enter a convent. Yet what, she wondered, would she do with the rest of her life?

With no husband or children, Jeanne was in an unusual position. Most wealthy European women of the time were not educated beyond basic reading and writing levels, and were expected to become mothers and housewives.

Guerrier Iroquois

Even though Canada's Aboriginal people had their own spirituality, European settlers wanted to spread their Christian faith.

It was at this crucial time that her cousin, Nicolas Dolebeau, a chaplain from Paris, visited Jeanne and told her about the work that missionaries were doing in New France (what we know as Québec today). Missionaries were people who wanted to spread the Catholic religion to the Aboriginal people of France's colonies in the new world. Her cousin's stories fascinated Jeanne. What a wonderful opportunity to use her nursing skills. Surely she could help the missionaries, and the Aboriginal peoples. Here was a chance to do something meaningful with her life.

Jeanne felt that she could not make such a weighty decision by herself. Being a religious person, she went to talk to her priest. He encouraged her to go to Paris to meet with the people who were in charge of sending missionaries to New France.

In Paris, Jeanne met Madame Angélique de Bullion, the widow of the king's former *financier* (the man who was in charge of the king's treasury). Madame de Bullion was very rich, and wanted to use some of her money to help the missionaries bring Catholicism to New France.

Until the 20th century, hospitals in Canada were institutions for the sick poor, as those able to pay doctors preferred to be treated at home.

The missionaries were planning to start a new settlement on Montréal Island, about 300 kilometres east of the French colony in Québec City. She asked Jeanne to go and supervise the founding of a hospital there. Madame de Bullion said she would provide the money if Jeanne would run the hospital. This was an enormous decision for Jeanne. It meant leaving everyone and everything she knew and loved in France to travel across a vast ocean to an unknown, unsettled, and dangerous land. After much thought, she agreed to go. It was, she believed, her destiny. She later wrote: "There is nothing in the world that I would refuse to do to accomplish the divine and all-loving will of God. It is the only desire and love of my heart. Therein is my passion, all my affections, my only love, and my sole paradise."

On May 9, 1641, Jeanne boarded a ship sailing for New France. Also on board was Paul de Chomedey de Maisonneuve, who had been hired to lead a group of settlers to establish the brand new colony on Montréal Island.

De Maisonneuve joined the French military in 1625 at the age of thirteen and was noted for his nobility as a soldier and his religious piety.

The Atlantic crossing was slow and rough. Wind and rain rocked the ship. Water swept across the decks. By the time they arrived in Québec City three months later in August, everyone was exhausted, and they decided to remain there through the winter. Jeanne spent the time caring for the people in the colony, and she and de Maisonneuve met with Charles Huault de Montmagny, who was the governor of New France. He warned that the Montréal expedition was a "foolhardy enterprise" and begged them to stay in Québec City. It was dangerous to settle in Montréal, he said, because the Iroquois who lived in the area were unfriendly and often attacked and killed settlers.

The Iroquois were firm allies of the British, and were openly hostile to French colonists until the French lost control of Canada in 1763.

The French settlement of Ville-Marie (later called Montréal) was located in a key region for the development of agriculture and the fur trade. Colonists intended to bring Christianity to the Aboriginal people living there.

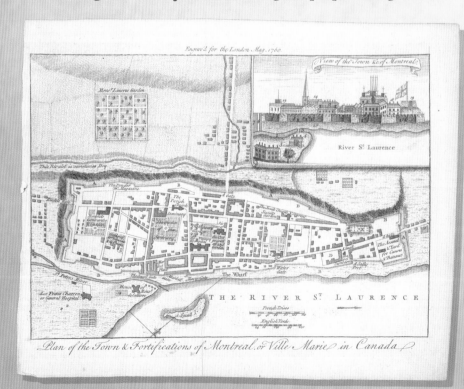

*Montréal means "Mount Royal." At first it referred only to the mountain on the island of Montréal, then to the island itself and, finally, to the settlement. The explorer Jacques Cartier first used the expression on his second voyage to New France in 1535. When Jeanne Mance and de Maisonneuve arrived, they named the settlement Ville-Marie, in honour of the Virgin Mary who was the protectress of their venture. However, people continued to call the settlement Montréal and it eventually became the city's official name.*

In spite of the governor's warnings, de Maisonneuve was determined to complete the job for which he had been hired. He waited until spring and then he, Jeanne, and a group of missionaries left Québec City. On May 17, 1642, they founded the settlement of Ville-Marie, which later became the city of Montréal.

As soon as they arrived, Jeanne got to work. She set up a hospital, the Hôtel-Dieu de Montréal, in a tent. The missionaries built a wall to protect the settlement from both the Iroquois and the waters of the St. Lawrence River. The following winter, when the river flooded, the wall kept out the raging waters. In thanks, de Maisonneuve, Jeanne, and the other settlers planted a wooden cross on the top of Mount Royal. A brightly lit cross still shines on the same spot today.

In 1645, Jeanne supervised the building of a more permanent wooden structure for the hospital. It was a single long room with a fireplace at one end that was used for cooking and heating. It had eight beds: six for men and two for women (because there were so few women living in the settlement). A small upstairs room served as living quarters, and an adjoining attic was used to dry laundry. Supplies such as medical instruments, linens, and furniture for the chapel were shipped from France.

When Jeanne Mance became a nurse, she did not go through a formal training program as nurses do today. In France, she learned to treat patients by watching what the other nurses and doctors did.

The Roman Catholic church sent missionaries to New France to educate the settlers and to bring Christianity to the Aboriginal people. Catholicism took hold slowly but gained a solid presence in time.

Life in Montréal was difficult. Jeanne and the colonists had to deal with floods, bitterly cold winters, disease, and frequent attacks by the Iroquois, who killed many of the settlers and burned their houses. Jeanne herself was almost taken prisoner several times and was often in the middle of ferocious battles. In spite of the turmoil, she tended her patients with loving care. She cleaned wounds and prepared medicines and salves. She planted gardens of medicinal plants such as feverfew, camomile, and lavender, and treated anyone who was sick or wounded, whether they were French or Aboriginal. Her patients called her "the Angel of the Colony."

## Medicine in the 1600s

*Medical care was very different when Jeanne Mance was nursing. In those days, nurses washed patients, comforted them, fed them, and dressed their wounds with bandages. Germs had not yet been discovered so no one worried about keeping bandages and medical instruments clean and sterile. Sometimes they used salt water or herbal concoctions to wash wounds. Prayer was often a major part of the healing process. At that time people believed that diseases were caused by imbalances in the body. Bleeding a patient was a common treatment. This was done by using leeches (bloodsucking worms found in some rivers and lakes) to draw blood and with it, they thought, the bad "humours," or imbalances, that were making the patient sick. Medicines were herbs, sometimes brewed into herbal teas. Occasionally dried medicinal herbs were rolled into "pills" that patients swallowed. People suffered from a wide range of serious diseases. These included smallpox, cholera, typhus, tuberculosis, and measles. Most of these diseases were unknown in the New World until Europeans introduced them. When Aboriginal people caught any of these illnesses, they usually died because they did not have natural resistance to them. Thousands were wiped out by measles, smallpox, and other diseases that colonists brought with them.*

In addition to her hospital duties, Jeanne oversaw the financial needs of the colony. An agreement signed in Paris on March 17, 1648, named Jeanne as the administrator of the Hôtel-Dieu du Montréal and stipulated that she would remain so until her death. On three occasions, when the colony was endangered by lack of funds, she made the dangerous sea voyage back to France to raise money, recruit nuns to work with her, and find ways of ensuring that future funds and resources would be sent to the new settlement of Montréal.

Marguerite Bourgeoys, a nun from France, arrived in New France in 1653. She opened her first school for girls in 1658, and went on to open others, including a school for Aboriginal girls.

## The French and Iroquois Wars

*The French and Iroquois Wars are also called The Beaver Wars because in the mid-1600s the Iroquois wanted to rule the beaver fur trade. They had come to rely on the money they earned from the fur to buy guns and other goods from European traders. That meant controlling the territory along the St. Lawrence River and the Great Lakes. The Iroquois were very fierce and much-feared fighters. The Algonquins called them Irinakhoiw, which means rattlesnake. The French added the ois to make their name Iroquois. At first they attacked the villages of the Hurons, an Algonquin tribe who lived in the region. In the 1640s they began attacking the French. The raids were vicious. The warriors would swoop out of the woods, murder the settlers, and burn their farms to the ground. It wasn't until the late 1600s that the French brought in soldiers who could fight back against the Iroquois.*

In 1650, Jeanne returned from her first trip to France to find the colony in serious peril. Attacks by the Iroquois had increased, and many colonists had been killed. Jeanne made a daring decision that allowed the colony to survive. She authorized the use of 22,000 livres (one livre equalled a pound of silver) of hospital funds to be used to recruit new colonists to defend the settlement. De Maisonneuve took the money and sailed to France. He returned with 100 settlers, four priests, and Marguerite Bourgeoys, a nun who became Jeanne's best friend and, eventually, Canada's first saint.

In January 1656, Jeanne slipped on ice; she fractured her right arm and dislocated her wrist. In spite of the serious injury and pain, she travelled as planned to France and returned with three nuns—Judith Moreau de Bresoles, Catherine Mace, and Marie Maillet—who formed the religious order of the Hospitalliers of St. Joseph, which still exists today.

Although Jeanne never married, she collected a large and loving family. She cared for many orphans and acted as godmother to over 40 children. For thirty years, Jeanne dedicated her life to the hospital. Eventually, however, the effort and her tireless determination wore her down. She became ill and died at the hospital she had founded, in June 1673, at the age of 67. She left behind a strong, self-sufficient settlement that became the great city of Montréal.

The Hôtel-Dieu Hospital is still a working hospital in the modern city of Montréal.

# Josiah Henson

## Champion of Freedom

Josiah looked up at the people shouting at him from the shore. Black and white, they all had the same message: "Stay here and be free." What should he do? His head was spinning. He had given his word to his master, Isaac Riley, to deliver eighteen slaves, including himself and his family, to Riley's brother in Kentucky. To get there, they were sailing through Ohio, a slave-free state. He could dock the boat and liberate his companions. He could take his wife and children to freedom; perhaps some day own his own house and land. Yet he had given his master his word. The shouts from shore were getting louder. His charges were waiting for his decision. They trusted him. So did Riley, his master. What should he do?

Josiah Henson was born a slave on June 15, 1789, the youngest of a family of six children. He lived on a Maryland plantation where his mother, Celia, had been hired out by her owner, Dr. McPherson. Josiah's earliest memory was seeing his father carried into their cabin, his back striped with bloody whip marks, more blood streaming from the spot where his ear had been cut off. His crime was trying to protect Celia from an attack by the plantation's white overseer.

After the whipping, Josiah's father was sold, and Celia and the children were sent back to Dr. McPherson's plantation. When the doctor died three years later, his brother put the slaves up for sale. Josiah never forgot the horror of the slave auction, where he and his brothers and sisters were torn from their mother's arms. When Celia begged Issac Riley, the man who bought her, to at least buy Josiah too, Riley kicked and beat her until she crawled away in agony.

Slaves worked all day for their masters, most never earning any money of their own.

Josiah was bought by Merton Robb, a tavern keeper. Robb was a cruel master who mistreated his slaves. Josiah was always hungry and cold and soon became seriously ill. Robb thought Josiah was going to die so he sold him to Riley. Josiah was ecstatic to be reunited with his mother, and under her care, he quickly recovered from his illness. Riley, though, was also a brutal man who abused his slaves. Josiah slept with ten others on the dirt floor of a leaky wooden cabin. There was little food and no beds or furniture, yet somehow Josiah grew up strong and healthy.

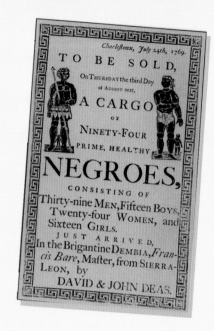

Slaves were bought and sold at auctions, treated as property and not as people.

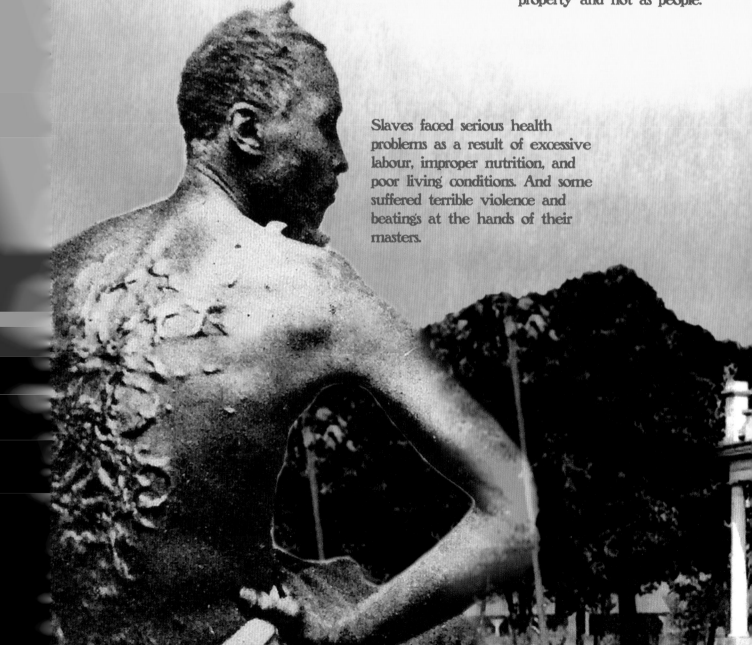

Slaves faced serious health problems as a result of excessive labour, improper nutrition, and poor living conditions. And some suffered terrible violence and beatings at the hands of their masters.

When he was 18, Josiah met John McKenny, a white preacher who hated slavery. Under McKenny's guidance, Josiah became a devout Christian. He began preaching to other slaves who soon looked up to him as their leader. He preached from memory because, like all slaves, Josiah could neither read nor write. When he was 22, he married Charlotte, a slave girl he met at a church meeting.

Because of Josiah's quick mind and strong body, Issac Riley made Josiah his bodyguard. Riley was a heavy drinker and gambler. Eventually he lost all of his money. When he learned that his slaves were going to be sold to pay his debts, Riley had Josiah quickly take them away to his brother Amos's plantation in Kentucky. To get there, the group passed through Ohio, a slave-free state, where Josiah could have set his charges free. Instead, he delivered them, as he had promised, to Amos Riley. It was a decision he regretted for the rest of his life.

Slaves received no education. Schools, like this one, were only available once a slave was freed.

Josiah began to plan to be free. He approached Amos Riley, who agreed to allow him to buy his freedom for $450. To pay, Josiah gave him his horse, and all the money he'd raised by preaching. However, he learned that Riley had tricked him by changing the amount to $1000. Then he learned that Riley planned to sell him.

Any slave who escaped was in great danger of being caught and returned for a reward, as shown in the ad above.

The *Song of the Free* was sung by slaves on the Underground Railroad, reminding them of the prospect of freedom not far away.

## SONG OF THE FREE.

TUNE—Susannah.

I'm on my way to Canada,
    That cold and dreary land,
The dire effects of slavery
    I can no longer stand,
My soul is vexed within me sore
    To think that I'm a slave,
I'm now resolved to strike the blow
    For freedom or the grave.
Oh, righteous father, wilt thou not pity me,
And aid me on to Canada, where colored men are
    free.

I heard the Queen of England say
    If we would all forsake
Our native land of slavery
    And come across the lake,
That she was standing on the shore
    With arms extended wide,
To give us all a peaceful home
    Beyond the rolling tide.
Farewell old master, that's enough for me,
I'm going straight to Canada where colored men
    are free.

Grieve not my wife,
    Grieve not for me,
Oh, do not break my heart;
    For nought but cruel slavery
Would cause me to depart,
    If I should stay to quell your grief,
Your grief I would augment,
    For no one knows the day that we
Asunder may be rent.
Oh, Susannah don't cry after me,
I'm going up to Canada where colored men are
    free.

I served my master all my days
    Without a dime's reward,
But now I'm forced to run away
    To flee the lash abhored,
The hourds are baying on my track
    The master just behind,
Resolved that he will bring me back
    Before I cross the line.
Oh, old master don't come after me            [free.
I'm going up to Canada where colored men are

I heard old master pray last night,
    I heard him pray for me,
That God would come and in his might
    From Satan set me free,
So I from Satan would escape
    And flee the wrath to come,
If there's a fiend in human shape
    Old Master must be one.
Oh, old master while you pray for me
I'm doing all I can to reach the land of liberty.

Ohio's not the place for me,
    For I was much surprised,
So many of her sons to see
    In garments of disguise;
Her name has gone throughout the world
    Free labor, soil and men,
But slaves had better far be hurled
    Into a lion's den.
Farewell Ohio, I'm not safe in thee,
I'll travel on to Canada where colored men are
    free.

I've now embarked for yonder's shore,
    Where man's a man by law,
The vessel soon will bear me o'er
    To shake the Lion's paw;
I no more dread the auctioneer,
    Nor fear the master's frown,
I no more tremble when I hear
    The baying negro hound.
Oh, old master, don't come after me,
I'm just in sight of Canada, where colored men
    are free.

I've landed safe in Canada,
    Both soul and body free,
My blood and brains and tears no more
    Shall drench old Tennessee;
Yet I behold the scalding tears
    Now streaming from my eye,
To think my wife, my only dear,
    A slave must live and die.
Oh, Susannah, don't grieve after me.
Forever at the throne of God, I will remember
    thee.

In desperation, Josiah decided to make the dangerous escape to Canada, where slavery was illegal. To do this, he, Charlotte, and their four children relied on Josiah's friends in Ohio and the Underground Railroad, the network of abolitionists who helped escaping slaves. Travelling by night, exhausted, frightened, and hungry, they slowly, painfully, made their way from Kentucky all the way to New York. From there, on October 28, 1830, they crossed the Niagara River into Canada. On landing, Josiah jumped from the boat and kissed the ground shouting, "I am free; I am free!"

*I am free; I am free.*

## The Underground Railroad

*The Underground Railroad was made up of people, black and white, who were opposed to slavery. They helped slaves escape from the South to the northern United States and Canada. These people provided food, safe houses where fugitives could rest, transportation, and encouragement. The term "underground," refers to the fact that the network was secret. It was called a "railroad" after the new train lines that were being built to move people around the country. Between 1810 and the start of the Civil War in 1861, the Underground Railroad helped about 100,000 slaves escape to freedom.*

Josiah's first Canadian employer, Mr. Hibbard, gave the family an empty barn that they turned into a comfortable home. He taught Josiah's son, Tom, to read. Tom, in turn, taught Josiah so he could read the Bible for himself. Now Josiah wanted to help others.

Josiah became a conductor on the Underground Railroad, and over the next few years smuggled 118 slaves into Canada. As more and more fugitive slaves settled in Upper Canada (Ontario), Josiah organized a group to establish a community where they could develop their skills and own their own land. It was called the Dawn Community.

*"Those who deny freedom to others deserve it not for themselves."*

~Abraham Lincoln

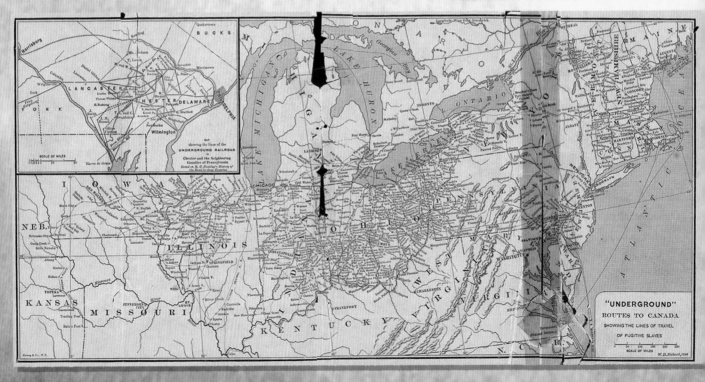

This map of the Underground Railroad shows the routes (in red) travelled by fugitive slaves.

## Freedom to Learn

*While escaped slaves in Canada were given full freedom, their children were not allowed to attend white schools. Josiah Henson believed that education was the key to true freedom. Together with Owen Wilson, a white abolitionist, he set out to establish schools for black children. By 1839, there were ten schools for fugitive slaves in Upper Canada.*

By the 1840s, Father Josiah, as he was now called, had become a well-known preacher and anti-slavery spokesperson whose work took him all over Ontario and the northern United States. Abolitionists in the North were pressuring the United States government to outlaw slavery everywhere in the country. The Southern states threatened to form their own country if that happened. Tempers ran high on both sides of the conflict.

On one visit to the United States, Josiah met Harriet Beecher Stowe, a writer who was interested in the abolitionist movement. A short time later she visited Josiah in Canada and recorded his story, which she used as the basis for her book, *Uncle Tom's Cabin*. The book ignited a firestorm of protest against slavery. U.S. President Abraham Lincoln later credited it as the spark that ignited the Civil War and ended slavery in the United States. Josiah, too, became famous as the real Uncle Tom, the book's central character.

Stowe's influential novel, *Uncle Tom's Cabin*, helped to raise awareness of the brutality of slavery. It reached millions of people as a novel and as a play, and was translated into dozens of languages.

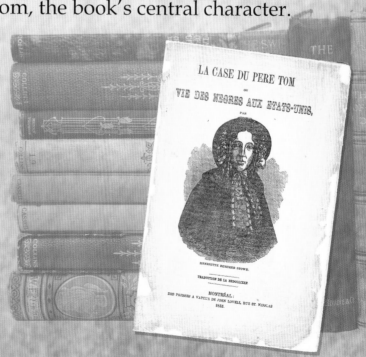

By 1850, so many slaves had crossed into Canada that the school in Dawn was overcrowded and in financial trouble. Josiah decided to raise money by selling the beautiful black walnut furniture the students were making from the trees surrounding the settlement. He took samples to the World's Fair in England, where he met many important people, including Queen Victoria, who stopped by his booth to admire his students' work. Josiah's joy was cut short, however, by an urgent request to return home. His wife Charlotte was seriously ill. Sadly, she died only a few weeks after his return. Josiah was devastated by his closest companion's death. They had been married for over 50 years.

Josiah Henson and his second wife, Nancy Gambril Henson (above, in 1877).

Two years after Charlotte died, Josiah married Nancy, a widow from Baltimore. With her, he made one last trip to England in 1877. *Uncle Tom's Cabin* had made him a public hero, and throngs of people came to see him wherever he spoke. Queen Victoria invited Josiah and Nancy to visit her at Windsor Castle. On their return to North America, they met with U.S. President Rutherford B. Hayes at the White House.

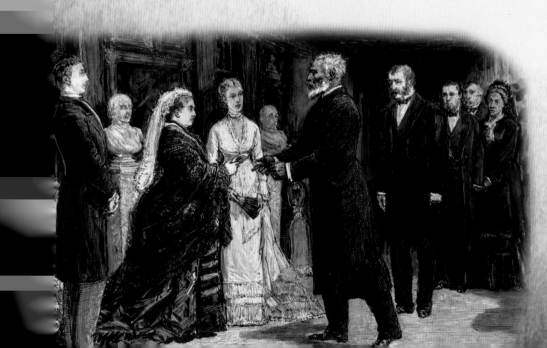

Henson made several trips to the British Isles, where he had the opportunity to meet Queen Victoria.

One hundred years after his death, Josiah Henson was honoured on a postage stamp.

Canada 32

Josiah Henson 1789-1883

postage/postes

In April 1883, Josiah Henson died at the age of 92 at his home in Dawn, Ontario. In 1983 he was honoured by being the first person of African descent to be featured on a Canadian postage stamp.

Josiah's descendents visit his tombstone.

# Nellie McClung
## Women Are Persons

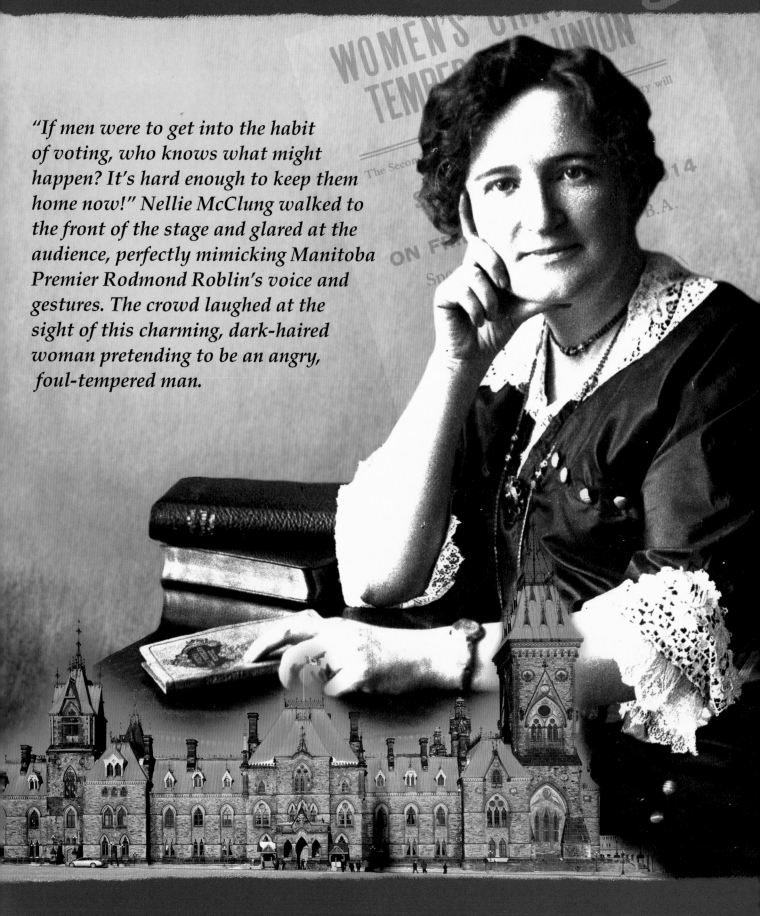

"If men were to get into the habit of voting, who knows what might happen? It's hard enough to keep them home now!" Nellie McClung walked to the front of the stage and glared at the audience, perfectly mimicking Manitoba Premier Rodmond Roblin's voice and gestures. The crowd laughed at the sight of this charming, dark-haired woman pretending to be an angry, foul-tempered man.

Even as a child, Nellie McClung wanted to help people. In 1888, at the age of 15, she left her family's farm in Ontario and moved to Somerset, Manitoba, to become a schoolteacher. The town had no money for a salary, so Nellie was paid only room and board. In 1896, she married Wes McClung, the son of the local Methodist minister, and had five children. She was a dedicated wife and mother, yet she still found time to be active in women's organizations. She also loved to write, and published her first novel, *Sowing Seeds in Danny*, in 1908.

Nellie McClung with her son, Tom, and dog, Philip, in the front yard of their home.

Always a sensitive person, Nellie saw the difference between her own busy, happy home life and those of less fortunate women. In the late 1800s and early 1900s, many men believed, and the law stated, that women were their husband's personal property. When a woman married, everything she owned, even her clothes, became her husband's property. He controlled their children and if he got drunk and beat his family, there were no laws to stop or punish him. Even if a woman worked beside her husband on a farm or in a business for many years, the money was all his and he could leave her destitute. Because women could not vote, there was no way they could change the law.

Nellie's home in Calgary, Alberta.

Nellie (right) with Emmeline Pankhurst, a British women's rights activist, who led the movement to win the right for women to vote in Britain.

By 1911, groups demanding the vote for women were springing up all over Canada and the United States. These women were called suffragists or suffragettes, from the word suffrage, which means, "to vote." Many women also wanted to pass a temperance law to ban alcohol. If men could not buy alcohol, they reasoned, they would not spend all the money they earned on liquor, get drunk, and then beat their wives and children. In Manitoba, Nellie was active in both movements through organizations such as the Women's Christian Temperance Union and the Political Equality League.

Unlike most women, Nellie earned her own money. *Sowing Seeds in Danny* was a big success, and she followed it with 15 more books. In the late 1800s, women were expected to stay home and care for their children, but Nellie hired household help. Many people, mostly men, said she ignored her children for the sake of her work. Nellie and her family, who knew how well she cared for her children, ignored the charges.

Since the adoption of the Canadian Charter of Rights and Freedoms in 1982, universal voting rights are protected in Canada through constitutional law.

Nellie became a dynamic speaker. She addressed church and civic groups and met with politicians to promote her causes. Her toughest critic was the Premier of Manitoba, Rodmond Roblin. Roblin scoffed at the idea of allowing women to vote. He told Nellie that "nice" women did not want the vote. Nellie replied: "By nice women. . .you probably mean selfish women who have no more thought for the underprivileged, overworked women than a pussycat in a sunny window for the starving kitten in the street. Now in that sense I am not a nice woman, for I do care." Roblin also told Nellie: "I don't want a hyena in petticoats talking at me. . . I want a nice, gentle creature to bring my slippers." Nellie eventually turned those words against him. She wrote a satirical play called *Why Men Should Have the Vote* in which she and the women of the Political Equality League ridiculed Roblin. One of the lines, "If men were to get into the habit of voting, who knows what might happen? It's hard enough to keep them home now," showed how pompous Roblin sounded and made the audience roar with laughter.

Nellie's tireless campaigning bore fruit. On January 27, 1916, the Manitoba Parliament passed the Bill for the Enfranchisement of Women under Roblin's successor, T. C. Norris. This made Manitoba the first province in Canada to give women the vote. Other provinces soon followed, and Canadian women received the federal vote in 1918. In Quebec, however, women were not allowed to vote or hold office until 1940, and women of Asian and First Nations descent did not gain the right to vote until the late 1940s, after World War II.

The Alberta Legislature in session, Edmonton, Alberta.

Nellie and her family moved to Edmonton, Alberta, in 1914, where she continued her political activities. She joined the Edmonton Equal Franchise League, which fought for women's rights, prohibition, and factory safety legislation. In 1921, she ran for and was elected to the Alberta Legislature and served one term. She lost her bid for re-election by 60 votes because of her continued support for prohibition.

Nellie became involved in the "Persons Case," one of the most famous legal cases in Canadian history. Another activist, lawyer Emily Murphy, was a suffragist who fought to have women declared "persons" in Canada. In 1916, the governor of Alberta had appointed Emily as a judge in women's court. On her first day, a lawyer, Eardley Jackson, challenged her right to be a judge because, he said, she was not considered a "person" under the British North America Act (BNA) of 1867. His objection was over-ruled by the Alberta Supreme Court.

A poster advertising the annual meeting of the Women's Christian Temperance Union (WCTU) in Calgary, Alberta.

# The British North America Act

*The British North America Act (BNA) was passed by the British Parliament in 1867. It is the law that united the Canadian provinces into one country, with a federation consisting of two main levels of government—provincial and federal.*

Though she was elated by the Alberta decision, Emily wanted all Canadian women to be considered "persons." In 1927, she decided to take her case to the Canadian Supreme Court. Emily invited Nellie and other activists, Henrietta Muir Edwards, Louise McKinney, and Irene Parr, to help her with her fight.

In August of that year, "The Famous Five," as they became known, asked the Supreme Court of Canada to consider whether the word "persons" in the BNA included women. The Court answered that women were not politically active in 1867 when the Act was written, and were, therefore, not considered "persons." The group then took their case to the Judicial Committee of England's Privy Council, at that time the highest Court of Appeal for Canada. On October 18, 1929, the Judicial Committee stated that "the word 'persons' includes both the male and female sex." This landmark decision affected women in Canada and throughout the British Empire from that day onwards.

The Famous Five, at the unveiling of a bronze tablet in their honour at the lobby of the Canadian Senate, Ottawa, 1938.

# Women in the Senate

*Until 1970, the Senate approved all divorces in Canada. The Famous Five believed that women would never be treated fairly until there were female Senators. Cairine Wilson became Canada's first female Senator in 1930, a few months after the Persons Case. It was 23 years until another woman, Iva Campbell Fallis, was appointed to the Senate.*

Nellie continued to work for women's rights for the rest of her life. She held many positions that were "firsts" for a Canadian woman. These included being appointed the first woman member of the Canadian Broadcasting Commission (CBC) Board of Broadcast Governors in 1936. In 1938, she was the sole female member of Canada's delegation to the League of Nations in Geneva, Switzerland (an organization established after World War I to prevent future wars, it was the forerunner to the United Nations). Each of these "firsts" set precedents for other women to follow. And slowly they did, first just a few, but then in their hundreds and thousands.

Nellie McClung was at the forefront during a time of great change for women. Though many men felt challenged and opposed change, Nellie and the women she worked with kept up the fight for rights that women take for granted today.

By the time she died in 1951 at age 78, Nellie was revered across Canada for her writing, her humanitarian work, and her insistence on fair treatment for all people.

"Never retract, never explain, never apologize; get things done and let them howl."

~ Nellie McClung

# Lester B. Pearson
## A Man of Peace

Lester B. Pearson looked out at the audience of elegantly dressed people that had come to honour him. The winner of the 1957 Nobel Peace Prize, Pearson was in the Oslo City Hall in Norway to accept the award. How had he, the son of a small-town minister, arrived at such a lofty position? He glanced at his speech. He had thanked the committee and the people of Norway. He had praised the legacy of Alfred Nobel, the man who had willed his estate to the pursuit of peace. Now it was time to conclude by sharing his dream for the future of the world. He took a deep breath. This, he knew, was the most important part of his speech.

When Lester B. Pearson, or "Mike" as he preferred to be called, was born in Toronto in 1897, there was nothing to indicate the dramatic turns that his life would take. His father, Edwin, was a Methodist minister who worked in small Ontario towns. His mother, Annie, was the bedrock of the family: baking, cooking, sewing—and raising her three lively boys with a firm hand and lots of love. Lester's childhood was filled with family, church, and sports. He was a fun-loving person with a warm, contagious smile and sharp sense of humour. These qualities would prove invaluable throughout his life, in his roles as a leader and peacemaker.

Lester was a great athlete who excelled at all sports.

In 1913, at the age of 16, Lester enrolled at the University of Toronto. When World War I broke out in 1914, he was too young to enlist in the military, so he volunteered to serve with a hospital unit and spent time overseas in England, Egypt, and Greece. When he was old enough, he transferred to the Royal Flying Corps, where he relished his training as a pilot. It was there that he got the nickname of "Mike," when his commanding officer told him that "Lester" was an unsuitable name for a fighter pilot. Lester, who liked being informal, decided that Mike was better than Lester and, for the rest of his life, that's what he told people to call him.

As a pilot in the war, Lester survived a plane crash only to be badly injured when he was hit by a bus while crossing a street during a blackout in London. Discharged from the military after he recuperated, Lester returned to Toronto, re-entered the university, and earned his Bachelor of Arts degree. After the war, Lester won a scholarship to Oxford University back in England. He then returned to Canada to teach history at the University of Toronto. In 1925, Lester married Maryon Moody, a young woman he first met when she attended one of his classes at the university. They settled into the quiet campus life of a university couple.

In 1928, Lester left the university to join the Canadian government's newly formed Department of External Affairs. The new department handled all of Canada's relations with other countries. This included business as well as diplomatic affairs. Until then, Canada's foreign affairs were mostly handled through Britain. When Mackenzie King became prime minister, he established the Department of External Affairs so that Canada could act on its own behalf, as an independent nation. Lester joined the department at this important point in time.

In those days, people joining the department took an exam. Lester scored highest, and was notified that he had been appointed First Secretary, or head of the department. The Pearsons moved to Ottawa, where their children, Geoffrey and Patricia, were born. For the next twenty years, Lester was actively involved in the growth of the Department of External Affairs. He did such a good job that, in recognition of his contribution, he received an Order of the British Empire. Lester hated any kind of pomp or formality, so instead of getting his award in an official ceremony, he insisted that the Governor General's assistant toss it to him over the net on a tennis court.

Lester's passion for sports and his disdain for formality stayed with him through his political career.

36

In 1935, Lester was sent to London, England, where he served in the office of the High Commissioner for Canada. This is the office that handles Canada's trade and political relations with Britain. He remained there when World War II broke out in 1939, and was in London during the worst part of the German bombing. He returned to Ottawa in 1941, and a year later was appointed Canada's Ambassador to the United States in Washington, D.C.

The Pearsons represented Canada at many diplomatic events.

## The United Nations

*In 1945, the world was recovering from the devastation of World War II. Many countries wanted to form an organization that would prevent such a war from ever happening again. U.S. President Franklin D. Roosevelt coined the name United Nations (UN). In 1945, 50 countries met in San Francisco and drew up the UN charter. The charter set out the rules and goals of the new organization. These include getting nations to settle disagreements peaceably, instead of going to war, and promoting basic human rights. The UN charter states that all people have the right to life, liberty, and the security of person; that no one should be held in slavery; that everyone is entitled to fair treatment under the law; and that people should be allowed to emigrate from one country to another.*

In 1948, Lester's life took another sharp turn when he decided to enter federal politics. As a member of the Liberal party, he ran for — and won — the riding of Algoma-East in Ontario. Prime Minister Louis St. Laurent immediately appointed Lester Minister of External Affairs.

Lester used his position to promote his ideals of peace and security. He drafted the speech in which St. Laurent proposed establishing the North Atlantic Treaty Organization (NATO). Lester signed the treaty in 1949 and headed the Canadian NATO delegation until 1957. He also headed the Canadian delegation to the UN from 1946 to 1956 and was elected president of the UN General Assembly for the 1952–53 session. His leadership helped establish Canada's reputation as an international peacemaker. This reputation grew even stronger when Lester prevented a war over control of Egypt's Suez Canal.

Lester B. Pearson flashes a victory sign at photographers.

## North Atlantic Treaty Organization

After World War II, Canada, the United States, and western European nations were afraid of the Soviet Union's growing military power. They formed NATO as an alliance of countries that pledged to protect each other in case of an attack by another country. The original members were Belgium, Canada, Denmark, France, Iceland, Italy, Luxembourg, the Netherlands, Norway, Portugal, the United Kingdom, and the United States. Since then, NATO has grown to include 26 countries.

The Suez Canal is the only direct link between the Mediterranean and Indian Ocean. This makes it vital for trade between Asia, Europe, and Middle Eastern countries such as Egypt, Lebanon, Syria, Israel, and Jordan. When the canal opened on November 17, 1869, it was open to ships from all nations. That was to change, bringing Egypt and Israel to the brink of a war.

Gamal Abdul Nasser became president of Egypt in 1956. The British had been ruling Egypt, including the canal, for 75 years. Nasser and the Egyptian people wanted the British to leave their country. When the British finally departed in June 1956, Nasser set out to modernize Egypt. His first goal was to build the Aswan Dam, an enormous hydro-electric project that would harness the waters of the Nile River. This was a very expensive project, which the United States and Britain had promised to finance.

In July 1956, the U.S. government announced that it would not give Egypt the money for the dam because it did not believe that Egypt would be able to complete the project. When the U.S. backed out, Britain did too. In retaliation, Nasser took control of the Suez Canal. Nasser said that Egypt would use the money that ships paid to pass through the canal to build the dam. The move also allowed Egypt to say which ships could, and could not, use the canal. For example, they refused to admit Israeli ships or any ship taking goods to or from Israel. This created a blockade of Israel; since it could not send or receive the goods it needed by sea.

In response, French, British, and Israeli troops attacked Egypt, saying they wanted to keep the canal open to all countries. Egypt reacted by sinking the 40 ships that were in the canal at the time.

To avoid a war, Lester drafted a plan to set up the UN's first peacekeeping force, in the Canal Zone. The UN force allowed Egypt, England, France, and Israel to back away from the fight without losing face. It made sure the canal stayed open, and that Egypt and the invaders did not resume their fighting. In return, Egypt agreed to let international ships, including those going to and from Israel, use the waterway.

Peacekeeping soldiers watch over the Suez Canal, an important and strategic waterway in the Middle East.

In 1957, Lester won the Nobel Peace Prize for his successful strategy to avoid war in the Middle East. Lester was such a modest person, he had never thought about winning the prize. His response after hearing he had won was simply, "Gosh."

Lester B. Pearson is the only Canadian who has ever won a Nobel Peace Prize.

## From Lester B. Pearson's Nobel Prize Acceptance Speech:

*"Of all our dreams today, there is none more important — or so hard to realize — than that of peace in the world. May we never lose our faith in it or our resolve to do everything that can be done to convert it one day into reality."*

## The Maple Leaf

*Lester's most controversial act as prime minister was the creation of a national Canadian flag. John Diefenbaker, the leader of the opposition, wanted to keep the existing flag. This featured a version of Great Britain's Union Jack flag, and symbolized Canada's ties to Britain. Lester believed that Canada should have its own flag. In 1964, he appointed a committee to come up with a design. The winner was the Maple Leaf, our national symbol from then on.*

In 1957, the Liberal government was defeated. A few months after, Pearson was chosen to be the head of the Liberal party, making him the leader of the opposition. Six years after that, he became prime minister. During his five years in that post, he established many important social programs that greatly changed the lives of Canadians for the better. These include old age pensions, to give Canadians money to live on in their later years; the Order of Canada, to recognize people who do great things for their country; and universal health care, which gives all Canadians access to free medical treatment.

Lester retired as leader of the Liberal Party in 1968. He had spent his entire life working to better the lives of others. He died in 1972, and is remembered as a fun-loving, universally respected leader who eloquently and successfully promoted the ideals of peace, compassion, and human rights for Canada, and the rest of the world.

# Roger Obata
## *Fighting for Justice*

Roger Obata looked across the table at his childhood friends and his heart ached for them. Roger knew they were loyal Canadians just like himself. Yet they had been forced to abandon their homes and businesses and move with their families into internment camps where they were treated as prisoners. This had happened because they were of Japanese descent and Canada was at war with Japan. Even after the war ended they were branded as "enemy aliens" and forced to leave their home province of British Columbia. How could he help them? And how, he wondered, could he make other Canadians apologize for the wrong that had been done?

Roger (centre) and his brothers as young boys in British Columbia.

Roger Obata was born in Prince George, British Columbia, on April 20, 1915. He went to Canadian schools and graduated from the University of British Columbia with a degree in engineering. At the time, there was a great deal of prejudice against Japanese Canadians who lived in British Columbia. They could not work in professions such as engineering, law, education, pharmacy, accounting, or hold jobs with the government. Because he was not allowed to work in his profession, Roger had to move to Toronto, Ontario, where there were no laws discriminating against people of Japanese descent, to find a job.

# The First Japanese Person in Canada

*Although some shipwrecked Japanese sailors may have washed ashore before him, the first Japanese person to settle in Canada is recognized as Manzo Nagano. He arrived in 1877. Other immigrants followed. Most were men, seeking adventure, better living conditions, or freedom from restrictive families. The first Japanese woman, Yo Oya, arrived in Vancouver in 1887. In 1889, she became the mother of Katuji Oya, the first Nisei, or second-generation Japanese Canadian.*

Like all Canadians, Roger knew that Japan was preparing to go to war. In 1937, Japanese armies invaded China. At the same time, under Adolf Hitler's rule, Nazi Germany was also preparing for war. World War II started in Europe when Germany invaded Poland on September 1, 1939. On September 27, 1940, Germany, Italy, and Japan signed a pact called the Axis Alliance. This meant that Canada, which was already fighting Nazi Germany, was now also at war with Japan.

When World War II brought Canada and Japan into conflict, Japanese Canadians began to be viewed with suspicion and their loyalty called into question.

Families were torn apart as women, children, and the elderly were sent to internment camps far inland, while the men were sent to labour camps to build roads or work on railways.

In the spring of 1941, the Canadian government fingerprinted and photographed all Japanese Canadians over the age of 16 and made them carry identity cards. The government labelled all Japanese Canadians as "enemy aliens." Then in 1942, the government expelled 21,000 Japanese Canadians living within 100 miles of the British Columbia coast, and sent them to live in internment camps. British Columbia and Japan are located on opposite sides of the Pacific Ocean. The government feared that if Japan attacked Canada, those Japanese living near the coast might help them. Of those who were moved, 63% were born in Canada, and 14% of those who had immigrated had become Canadian citizens. None had committed acts of sabotage or acted as spies in any way.

All Japanese Canadians over the age of 16 had to carry official photo identity cards, with their fingerprints on the back.

The Bearer, whose photograph and specimen of signature appear hereon, has been duly registered in compliance with the provisions of Order-in-Council P. C. 117.

Vancouver
(Date) July 25th, 1941

Issuing
Officer

# Visibly Different

*Canada was at war with Germany, Italy, and Japan, yet only Japanese Canadians were labelled as enemy aliens. This action was a sign of the racism and discrimination that existed during the years leading up to and during World War II.*

Conditions in the internment camps were not like home. Some camps had tents; in others, people lived in unheated tar-paper shacks. During the winter, pipes froze, icicles dripped from the ceilings, and clothing and bedding became mildewed. Inmates were guarded night and day. Their mail was censored, they had to carry registration cards, and they could not leave the camp without a permit. Many family members were separated and sent to different camps. To make matters worse, the government seized their personal property, including fishing boats, homes, businesses, and land, and sold it. The owners received no money for the property they had worked hard to buy and maintain.

Though camps had stores and schools, the internees did not have the comforts and freedoms of home. But a spirit of community existed, with residents making the best of their situation.

The Japanese Canadian owners of these fishing boats lost their freedom, and all they had worked for.

Roger (far right) disagreed with the Canadian government's treatment of its Japanese Canadian citizens, but still felt a duty to serve his country alongside other Canadians.

Roger, who was living in Toronto at the time, escaped the evacuation because only the Japanese on the West Coast of Canada were affected. In spite of his anger about the treatment of Japanese Canadians, he enlisted in the Canadian army to help defeat the Axis powers. Roger had lived his whole life in Canada, and he also spoke fluent Japanese. Because of this skill, the army loaned him to the United States Intelligence Service in Washington, D.C., to translate wartime Japanese documents.

When he returned to Canada after the war, Roger met family and friends who had been released from the camps but thrown out of British Columbia. They had lost their homes, their businesses, and their pride. As they sat at café tables or in barely furnished apartments in Toronto, they talked about "redress." The Canadian government, they said, should repay them for what it had stolen. Roger agreed that they needed an organization that would fight for them.

Even after they were finally set free, the internees had no homes or businesses to return to. They may have had their freedom, but they had little else. Many Japanese Canadians—more than 4,000—chose to leave Canada. Obata and others wanted something done to compensate the innocent families.

# Japanese Canadians Denied Basic Human Rights

*The first Japanese Canadians who lived in Canada were allowed to become citizens; however, they were not allowed to vote. In 1931, the Japanese Canadian veterans of World War I were given the vote, but it wasn't until 1949 that all Japanese Canadians were granted the same right. This prejudice and lack of civil rights was the root cause of the Japanese internment camps and the eviction of Japanese Canadians from British Columbia during, and directly after, World War II.*

In 1947, Roger was elected founding president of the National Japanese Canadian Citizens' Association (later the National Association of Japanese Canadians, or NAJC). Their goal was to seek property claims from the federal government and to get the government to officially apologize for labelling them enemy aliens.

In 1950, the government appointed Supreme Court Justice Henry Bird to head a Royal Commission. Roger and his group had spent hundreds of hours examining property claims. The government, they calculated, owed them $15 million. The Bird Commission, however, authorized payments of only $1.25 million and demanded that anyone accepting the payment waive their right to all future claims. Roger thought the offer was an insult. It would be another 34 years before he realized his dream.

Redress rally on Parliament Hill in Ottawa, on April 14, 1988.

In 1977, Japanese Canadians gathered in Vancouver to mark the 100th anniversary of the arrival of Manzo Nagano, the first Japanese person to settle in Canada. As people talked, the subject of redress came up again and again. With Roger at the helm, the NAJC began a new redress campaign. Eleven years later, on September 22, 1988, Prime Minister Brian Mulroney signed the Redress Agreement. The agreement awarded over $300 million. Speaking before the House of Commons, Prime Minister Mulroney apologized for the government's wrongful actions. Most important to Roger and his group, Parliament removed the hated term "enemy alien," from all official records. As insurance that such a thing would never happen again, Parliament created the Canadian Race Relations Foundation, a national organization to promote racial harmony and help eliminate racism.

Roger (standing, left) receives a plaque acknowledging over 40 years of service with the NAJC.

Roger Obata was made a member of the Order of Canada in 1990, for his work on behalf of Japanese Canadians and his 41-year battle to right a grievous wrong.

It would take more than 40 years, but Roger finally saw his dream come true with the Canadian government's apology and compensation in 1988.

# June Callwood
## The Right to Live with Dignity

June Callwood looked at the young men sprawled on the sidewalk. They were living on the street because they had nowhere else to go. Many had dropped out of school and run away to Toronto. They were hungry, dirty, and often needed medical care. She knew that somehow she had to help them. Identifying the problem, June decided, was only the first step. The next was figuring out how to solve it. But how? The answer, she realized, was to create a refuge where these street kids could find food, shelter, and help in getting their lives together.

June Callwood did not set out to become a journalist or an activist, yet when she saw situations that needed action, she quickly made them her own. June devoted much of her life to helping others. As a journalist, she wrote about causes such as abused women, AIDS, child poverty, civil liberties, and teen mothers; as an activist, she embraced them.

From a young age, June understood hard times, and it helped develop in her a compassion for others.

June was born in Chatham, Ontario, in 1924. Her mother, Gladys Lavoie, was French Canadian. Her father, Harold (Byng) Callwood, was English Canadian.

In 1929, the Great Depression hit Canada and the United States. Byng lost the business he had started to repair farmers' tin milk cans, the Superior Tinning and Retinning Company. Unable to find work, he left his family and, like thousands of Depression-era men, went west to see what he could find. Gladys struggled to support June and her sister, Jane. At times she could not even pay the rent, and they had to sneak out of their house at night, to avoid the landlord. June wore used clothes and sometimes did not eat for several days. In later years, memories of these difficult times played a big part in her desire to help others.

In 1939, World War II started, and June's father signed on with the Royal Canadian Engineers. Gladys and the girls joined him in Regina, Saskatchewan, where he was training. When he went overseas in 1940, they returned to Ontario and settled in the town of Brantford, where June went to high school. But in her fourth year, Gladys made June quit school so she could help support her family through the hard times.

Although June was only 16 (she skipped three grades in elementary school), she got a job with the *Brantford Expositor*, a local newspaper. June edited stories by other reporters and wrote stories about soldiers at the local army camp. The hours were long. She worked six days a week, fifteen hours per day, and earned $7.50 a week.

June had always been a good writer. She had written for the school newspaper and had won a short-story contest. Her career as a journalist began at the young age of 16.

In 1942, the city editor of the *Toronto Daily Star* asked June to work for him for $25 a week. June was thrilled. She moved to Toronto and started her new job. Almost immediately, though, she got into trouble when a soldier questioned a caption she had written about an army tank. June's reply insulted the soldier, and when he complained to the editor, she was fired. June was devastated. How could she tell her family that she was out of work after only two weeks in Toronto?

Desperate for a job, June went to the *Globe and Mail*, the other big newspaper published in Toronto at the time. Gathering her courage, she walked into the office of Bob Farquharson, the editor. Mr. Farquharson was so surprised to see this eighteen-year-old girl standing in front of his desk that he gave her a trial assignment. He later hired her as a staff reporter.

The Globe and Mail

Banking & Finance

Business & Economy

June loved working for the *Globe*. She was earning a good salary, establishing a reputation as a writer, and making friends. One of these friends was another *Globe* reporter, Trent Frayne. She and Trent fell in love and were married on May 13, 1944. In those days, the *Globe* did not employ married women, so June kept the name Callwood for her by-line (the name on her articles).

She quit her job when she became pregnant with her first child, and became a freelance writer. From then on, June wrote for many different magazines and newspapers such as *Maclean's*, *Chatelaine*, and *Canadian Living*. Always adventurous, June even learned to pilot a plane, although she stopped flying when she was pregnant with her second child. In 1959, however, June flew again, when she wrote about the famous *Avro Arrow*.

June and Trent had four children altogether: Jill, Brant, Jennifer (later changed to Jesse), and Casey. Then, in the early 1950s, June suffered a devastating depression that left her unable to work. She had no energy; she felt unbearably sad and found herself staring out the window for hours at a time. Finally, June realized that she was sick and needed help. She sought therapy and recovered.

June had a lifelong passion for flying.

# The Avro Arrow

*The Avro CF-105 Arrow was designed to be one of the most advanced fighter airplanes ever built. It was designed and built by Avro Aircraft Limited (Canada) in Malton, Ontario, and was supposed to become the Royal Canadian Air Force's interceptor plane. June became involved with the story as a journalist, but also as a pilot, when the magazine Saturday Night sent her to Washington to write about the development of the Iroquois engine that had been developed for the Arrow by Orenda Engines. Always up to a challenge, June got into a flying suit and joined the crew that was testing the B-47 engine. In 1959, right after its test flight, the entire project was cancelled and many people lost their jobs. June wrote passionately and sensitively about the pilots and unemployed Avro Canada workers for the Toronto Daily Star.*

June and Trent, with son Casey.

However, that wasn't enough for her. As an investigative journalist, she wanted to learn the causes and treatment of the condition that had taken a year out of her life. She researched and wrote a book about depression called *Love, Hate, Fear, Anger and Other Lively Emotions*. Recovering from depression and then writing about it made June conscious of other people's suffering and how it could affect a person's life. She had discovered her passion—to write about and become active in causes that helped people in need. June became an "activist," a person who actively works to help others.

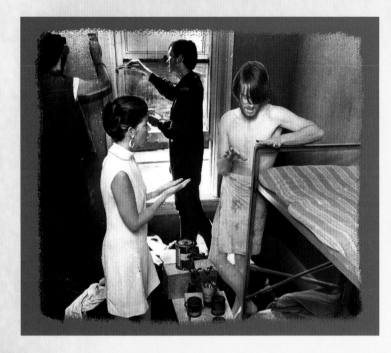

June speaks to a resident at Digger House. As an activist, June did not choose causes because they were popular; she chose to help people that the rest of society ignored.

In the late 1960s, June's eldest son, Brant, was living in the Yorkville area of Toronto. At the time, Yorkville was filled with young people. Many had dropped out of school or run away from home. Some were on drugs and living on the street. Sometimes Brant would bring one of these teens home for a meal. June fed them and gave them a place to sleep. She remembered what it was like to be poor and not have food or a decent place to live.

June wanted to find a way to help these street people change their lives. With help from Brant and other young people, she raised money to found a hostel for dropouts, runaways, and kids who were on drugs. They called it Digger House. The shelter opened in February 1968, and on the first night over 100 kids came to stay there. June opened other shelters for groups in need: Nellie's, a hostel for abused women, and then Jessie's, a place for pregnant teens and teen mothers to go for help and support.

Even as she worked to help others, June's own life was marked by tragedy. A cement mixer making an illegal turn hit their oldest daughter Jill on her bicycle. Doctors wanted to amputate Jill's left leg but, with her parents' help, she made a full recovery. Then in 1982, their youngest son, Casey, was killed when a car going the wrong way on a highway struck his motorcycle.

In spite of her grief, June continued to work for others. In the 1980s, AIDS had become a serious disease. Because it struck mostly young gay men at a time when there was a lot of prejudice toward homosexuality, people were ashamed to admit they had it. Many of these men were alone, because their families and friends had rejected them. June wanted to start an AIDS hospice — a homey, comfortable place where dying patients could be cared for, comforted, and helped to die in dignity. Casey House (named in honour of her son Casey) opened on March 1, 1988.

*"Give Compassion a Home"*

Casey House was the world's first AIDS hospice. Its motto is "Give Compassion a Home."

# The AIDS Epidemic

*In the 1970s, people started dying of a mysterious disease. At first, no one knew what it was. Then it was given a name: Auto Immune Deficiency Sydrome (AIDS). In the 1970s, an AIDS diagnosis was a death sentence. Today, there are drugs that help people live with the disease but there is still no cure. June was profoundly moved by the plight of the AIDS victims. Because no one knew how it was spread at first, people were afraid to associate with those who had the disease. Many of the victims found themselves desperately ill and alone. June felt that something had to be done. As an activist, she founded Casey House. As a journalist, she wrote about it in the newspaper and in two books:* **Jim: A Life with AIDS,** *and* **Trial Without End: A Shocking Story of Women and AIDS.**

Personal tragedy was not finished with June and her family. In 1993, Brant was diagnosed with multiple sclerosis and a dangerous aneurysm (a weak spot in an artery wall). Surgery to remove the aneurysm left him partly paralyzed. In spite of these personal tragedies, June continued her activism and her journalism, and also wrote dozens of books, under her own name and ghost-writing for others.

June lived by the belief that "If you see an injustice being committed, you're not an observer, you're a participant."

June never wanted thanks for her work. She helped start organizations, stayed involved, fund-raised, and fought for the causes she believed in. She fought for the right of all people to live with dignity. She was honoured many times for her good works. Her awards included B'nai Brith Woman of the Year, the City of Toronto Award (the highest civilian award given by the city), the Order of Ontario, the Order of Canada, the Toronto Arts Foundation Lifetime Achievement Award, and a Canadian Journalism Foundation Lifetime Achievement Award.

In November 2003, June was diagnosed with incurable cancer—there was nothing the doctors could do. When June heard the news she refused treatment. She said, "I don't like dependency. I'm just not going to be good at that. I hate the thought that I'd be taking people away from the things they really need to do."

She died on April 14, 2007, leaving behind a legacy of love, hope, and caring that touched thousands of lives.

June lived a life that set an example for others to follow.

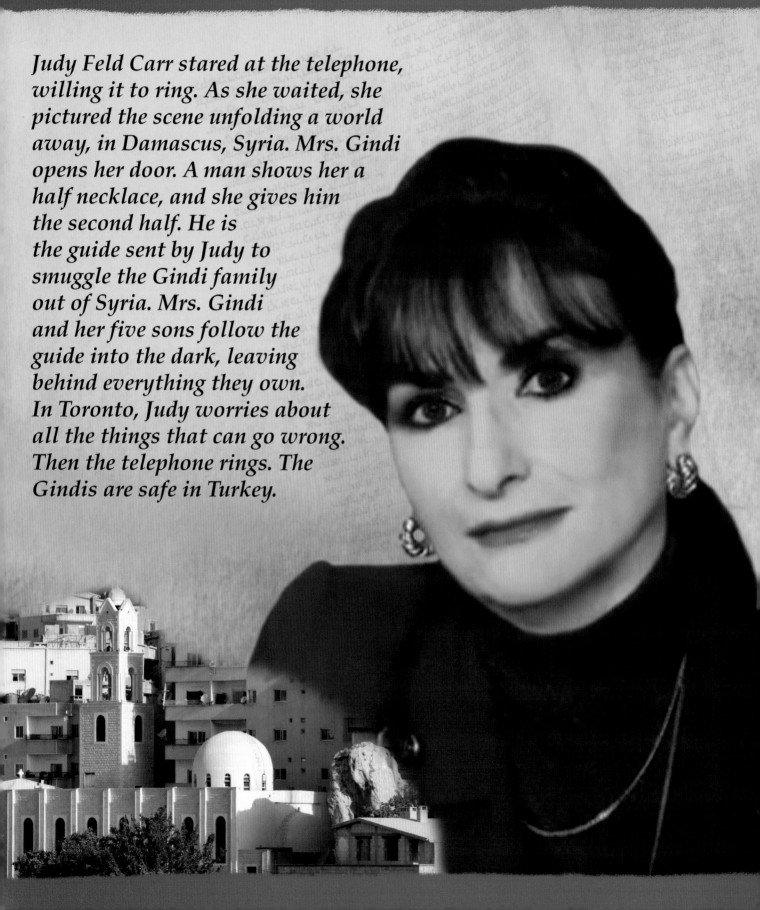

# Judy Feld Carr

## Living Safe and Free

Judy Feld Carr stared at the telephone, willing it to ring. As she waited, she pictured the scene unfolding a world away, in Damascus, Syria. Mrs. Gindi opens her door. A man shows her a half necklace, and she gives him the second half. He is the guide sent by Judy to smuggle the Gindi family out of Syria. Mrs. Gindi and her five sons follow the guide into the dark, leaving behind everything they own. In Toronto, Judy worries about all the things that can go wrong. Then the telephone rings. The Gindis are safe in Turkey.

For 25 years, Judy Feld Carr lived a double life. She cared for her family and taught music education in Toronto schools, all the while running a secret operation that rescued 3,228 Jews from a country where they lived under a brutal dictatorship that ruled over every aspect of their lives.

Judy (far right) brought thousands of families to safety, all the while living a "normal" life as a mother, wife, and teacher.

Judy was born in 1938 in Montreal and, at the age of five, moved with her family to Sudbury, Ontario. Her father, Jack Leve, was a fur trader who taught Judy how to be tough: to shoot a gun, to paddle a canoe, to catch and fillet fish, and, most important of all, how to be a proud Jew no matter what prejudice she faced.

There were few Jewish families in Sudbury in the 1940s, and Judy encountered anti-Semitism (prejudice because she was Jewish) at an early age. In 1947, when she was in grade two, a group of sixth graders called her "Christ killer" and knocked out her front teeth. That same year, a couple from Poland moved in next door. The woman, Sophie, was a Jewish Holocaust survivor who had been in the Auschwitz concentration camp where her first husband and her children were murdered. Sophie had been tortured, and as a result, could not have more children. She and Judy became fast friends—Judy was like a daughter to her. Judy made a promise that she would help make sure that Jews never again suffered as Sophie had. It was a promise she never forgot.

Judy loved music, and she left Sudbury to study music education and musicology at the University of Toronto. In her final undergraduate year, she met Ronald Feld, a doctor. The young couple were married a month after she graduated.

In 1972, Judy and Ronald read an article about the desperate living conditions of Jewish people in Syria. The country was ruled by a harsh dictator whose secret police, the Muhabarat, watched their every move. Their phones were tapped and their mail opened. Jews could not own cars or hold many types of jobs. They could be arrested and tortured for the slightest reason. Emigration (moving from one country to another) is a basic right as set out in the United Nations Declaration of Human Rights. Syrian Jews were denied that right. The more Judy read, the more horrified she became. Then she remembered her promise to Sophie.

## Jews in Syria

*There have been Jewish people living in Syria since Biblical times. In 636 AD, the Arab Muslims conquered Syria. Under their rule, Jews enjoyed many freedoms. When the Sephardic (Spanish) Jews were expelled from Spain in 1492, many came to Syria. At this time, Syria was part of the Ottoman Empire, which included what is today Turkey, Israel, Jordan, Lebanon, and Egypt. Under the Ottomans, Jews enjoyed freedom of religion.*

*After World War I (1914–1918), the Ottoman Empire fell and the French controlled Syria. Jews were still free to practice their religion. Life changed for Syrian Jews after the country gained its independence from France in 1946, following World War II. At that time, there were many attacks against Jewish people. Shops and synagogues were destroyed and thousands of Syrian Jews fled the country. Those who remained were denied their basic human rights. They could not own property, travel, or emigrate. If they tried to leave, they were arrested and often tortured. The plight of Syrian Jews went unnoticed until the 1970s when Judy Feld Carr took up their cause. Today there are only a handful of elderly Jews still living in Syria.*

The Felds decided to make contact with the Syrian Jewish community. In those days, you did not just pick up a telephone and call a foreign country. You had to place the call with an operator who contacted another operator in the country you were calling. The Felds met with Rabbi Serels of Toronto's Sephardic synagogue and placed the call from his office. The Canadian operator called an operator in Rome who put them through to an operator in Damascus. The operator in Rome asked to be put through to Rabbi Hamra, who was the leader of the Syrian Jewish community. The Syrian operator said there was no listing for such a person and hung up. The operator in Rome tried again but this time could not get through. The Canadian operator suggested they try again in a few days.

Something as seemingly simple as a telephone call took weeks to be successful.

It took almost three weeks before they succeeded and reached the Jewish school in Damascus. They asked to speak to Rabbi Hamra. The man who answered gave them a second phone number. This time they reached a man who lived next door to the rabbi. He asked the operator to call back within an hour and then ran to tell the rabbi about the call from Canada.

After World War II, Syrian Jews were persecuted, and their synagogues, like the Great Synagogue of Aleppo (right), were destroyed.

Rabbi Hamra knew that the Muhabarat had listened in on the call. So he went to the Muhabarat office and reported it. Then he went to his neighbour's house. When the phone rang, he spoke to Rabbi Serels who asked if Rabbi Hamra would welcome religious articles and books and asked for the address of the Jewish school so that he and his group could send the materials. He would confirm everything by telegram. After hanging up, Rabbi Hamra went back to the Muhabarat to tell them that he would be getting a telegram from Canada.

After that call, all communication with Syrian Jews was conducted by telegram. To fool the Muhabarat, the Felds used a secret code that was developed in the 1400s when Jews were persecuted in the Spanish Inquisition. It used biblical texts to hide the true meaning of a message.

## Quoting the Bible

*Passages from the Bible were used in coded telegrams. For example, after the Syrians staged a violent attack on the Jewish community, Judy received a telegram that said, "Rachel is weeping for her children." This told her that children had been hurt in the attack. When the Muhabarat questioned these passages, Rabbi Hamra explained that they were traditional Jewish greetings.*

In 1973, Ronald suffered a sudden heart attack and died. Judy was devastated. Suddenly she was a 33-year-old widow with three children to support. Judy juggled three teaching jobs, but continued her work on behalf of Syrian Jews. She could never give that up. In Ronald's honour, the board of governors of her synagogue, the Beth Tzedec Congregation in Toronto, set up the Dr. Ronald Feld Fund for Jews in Arab Lands. The money allowed Judy and friends to send more parcels of religious books and articles to the Jewish community in Syria.

In 1977, Judy married Donald Carr, a widower who also had three children. Donald was a lawyer and prominent member of the Canadian Jewish community. Judy continued her work on behalf of Syrian Jews. It was at this point that her life took a dramatic turn. Judy decided to become a rescuer.

Judy had learned that an elderly man, Toufik Srour, had bribed the Muhabarat to get a visitor's visa that let him go to the United States. If money could buy one man's freedom, she reasoned, it could buy freedom for others. But bribing people was dangerous. Everyone involved, from clerks, government officials, and judges, to members of the Muhabarat, had to be paid off. Judy did not know if these people could be trusted. She was putting the people she was trying to help in danger. If the Muhabarat discovered that they wanted to escape, they could be arrested, tortured, and even killed.

Though it was dangerous both for herself, and those she was reaching out to, Judy continued to work for Syrian Jews.

At the same time that Judy was arranging ransoms, she also arranged escapes. Ransoms meant getting one person out, but with escapes she could sometimes smuggle out a whole family. The escapes, however, brought serious problems. Who could she trust to take the money and actually deliver the people to safety? What routes were safe? And how could Judy know that her people were not being led into a trap? Judy knew that they were entrusting her with their lives and the lives of their children. She established a network of contacts, including a secret Syrian underground. The operation was very complicated. Everyone thought they were the only people working with her. Only Judy knew everyone who was involved

Helping a family like this one to flee the country was a complicated and dangerous process.

## *The Damascus Keter*

*When Judy learned that an ancient biblical text known as the Damascus Keter was hidden in the basement of the synagogue in Damascus, she wanted to get it out. This was an important historic and religious document and Judy knew that if it stayed in Syria, it would be lost or destroyed. She approached an Arabic-speaking Western businessman and asked him to bring her a package from Rabbi Hamra. She said it was a prayer book that the rabbi was sending her as a gift. The businessman, who suspected the package was more than a simple book, hid it among his business papers and smuggled it out of Syria. Judy was ecstatic. Shortly thereafter, Rabbi Hamra left Syria for good. He visited Judy in Toronto and asked her permission to take the Keter to Israel, where it is now housed in the National Library in Jerusalem.*

Judy kept records of everything she did, but never confided in anyone. However, with six bright, curious children in the house, it was impossible for her to keep her underground life a complete secret. The children knew about the rescues but knew not to talk of them. They learned to ignore the comings and goings of people who would appear for a few hours or days, and then disappear. If they guessed what their mother was doing, they never told anyone. The only people who knew about Judy's work were her husband, and her childhood friend, Helen Cooper, who worked with her.

In 1994, Syria allowed some of its remaining Jews to leave temporarily, but not permanently. Judy continued her work until she conducted her final rescue in 2001. It was only then, when she felt it was safe to do so, that Judy told her story.

To this day, most of the people that Judy rescued do not know who she is or even her full name. She is simply Mrs. Judy, the brave woman who saved them and their families from repression and danger, and brought them to new lives of freedom.

Judy has been given many honours and awards for her work. In 2001, she received the Order of Canada, the country's highest lifetime achievement award. Her favourite reward, however, is knowing that the thousands of people she rescued are living free and happy lives. And her favourite honour is the dozens of children born to them who are named Judy.

**Judy with Governor General Adrienne Clarkson.**

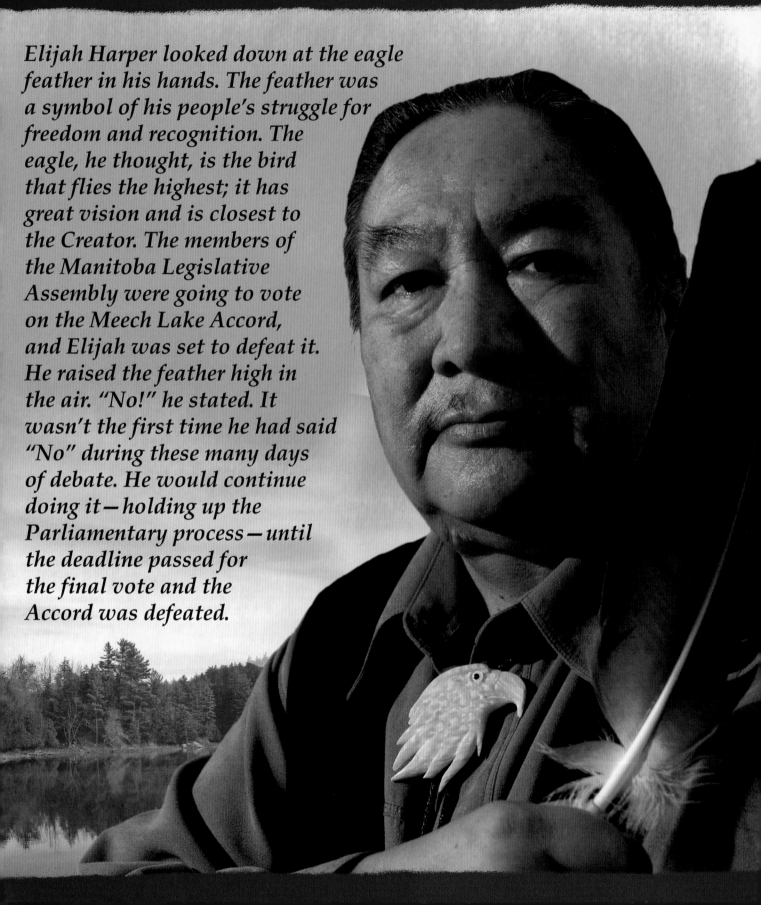

# Elijah Harper
## The Power of No

*Elijah Harper looked down at the eagle feather in his hands. The feather was a symbol of his people's struggle for freedom and recognition. The eagle, he thought, is the bird that flies the highest; it has great vision and is closest to the Creator. The members of the Manitoba Legislative Assembly were going to vote on the Meech Lake Accord, and Elijah was set to defeat it. He raised the feather high in the air. "No!" he stated. It wasn't the first time he had said "No" during these many days of debate. He would continue doing it — holding up the Parliamentary process — until the deadline passed for the final vote and the Accord was defeated.*

Imagine a peoples' whole world turned upside down so they could no longer live the way they had lived for hundreds of years. That's what happened to the Aboriginal people who lived in what is now Canada. When Europeans arrived, they slowly pushed the Aboriginal people off the lands, where they had hunted and trapped for many centuries. The newcomers brought diseases, such as measles, for which the Aboriginal people had no natural resistance. Tribes, or bands, were forced to live on cramped areas known as reserves and to obey the newcomers' laws. Their people lost their pride, their heritage and, too often, their lives. All of these things were in Elijah Harper's mind the day he denied the Meech Lake Accord in the Manitoba Legislature and uttered the word that forged Canadian history. That word was "No!"

## Columbus's Mistake

*It is thought the word "Indian" was first used by Christopher Columbus. Columbus sailed from Spain seeking an ocean passage to India. Instead, he sailed to the Caribbean and discovered the "New World." Thinking he was in India, he called the people living there Indians. Today, although it is still used, the term Indian is often considered an insult.*

Elijah Harper was born on March 3, 1949, in Red Sucker Lake, a Cree/Ojibway reserve in northern Manitoba. He was the second of thirteen children born to Allan B. and Ethel Harper. Both his father and grandfather lived off the land by hunting, fishing, trapping, and gathering. When Elijah was an infant, his parents gave him to his paternal grandparents, John E. Harper and Juliette, so they could raise him. This was common practice so the elders could teach children the ways of their people.

Life on the reserve was difficult, but people pitched in and helped each other. When someone hunted a moose or caught a fish, the entire community shared in the bounty. Yet there was also great poverty, overcrowding, and disease. Elijah, however, did not know he was poor. He loved living on the land. His happiest time was when he was in the bush trapping with his parents and grandfather.

# The Indian Act

The Indian Act of Canada was introduced in 1876. It gave the government control over most of the Aboriginal people and their land. In the 1700s, as European settlers took over the lands, the government began setting aside reserves where the Aboriginal people could live. The Indian Act gave the government the responsibility of caring for these reserves and the people living on them.

Under the act, Status Indians received government-funded education and health care. The government was responsible for keeping white settlers from trespassing on Indian land. However, while the act did have some positive sections, it contained many regulations that were not good for the Status Indians. They were not allowed to vote, have their own businesses, or own land. They could not leave their reserves without government permission. If a Status Indian wanted to become a Canadian citizen, he or she had to give up Indian status. And every reserve had a federal agent who worked for the Department of Indian Affairs. These agents controlled government money and had the final say on any decisions made by the reserve's own councils. The result was that, rather than integrating Aboriginal people into Canadian society, the Act isolated them by keeping them on their reserves.

In 1951, the power of the federal agents was reduced so that bands had more control over their own affairs. Aboriginal people were allowed to leave the reserve and to have businesses. In 1962 they won the right to vote in federal and provincial elections, and in 1985 people who left the reserve were no longer forced to give up their Indian status. While many Aboriginal people want to see the act abolished altogether, others believe that it protects some aspects of their culture and land. They would like greater self-government, while retaining some of the guaranteed benefits.

When Elijah was five he developed a lump under his chin. This was a symptom of tuberculosis, a serious and highly contagious lung disease that was common on the reserve due to the poor living conditions. In those days, government authorities were allowed to remove an Aboriginal child from his or her home without the family's permission. Elijah was put on a plane and flown to Norway House, a hospital on the northern tip of Lake Winnipeg. From there he was sent to The Pas, a tuberculosis sanatorium in Northern Manitoba. Suddenly he was in a hospital with strangers. He had no contact with his family.

Elijah recovered and returned home but when he was nine, he was taken away again. This time he was sent to the Residential School at Norway House on Lake Winnipeg, and later to the Brandon Residential School in Manitoba, where he stayed until he was sixteen. This was common practice for Aboriginal children. The government schools were run by churches. Children were removed from their communities and turned over to non-Aboriginal teachers who were supposed to "civilize" them by getting rid of all their Aboriginal customs. The teachers humiliated the children by shaving off their long hair and reading their mail. Children were not allowed to wear Aboriginal clothes, speak their own language, or practice their religion. They could not leave the school compound, other than to return to the reserve during the summer. Often they did not have adequate food or clothing and would become ill from the poor living conditions. Many children died.

The painful legacy of the residential schools has been felt for several generations. On June 11, 2008, a historic apology was issued by the Canadian government. Prime Minister Stephen Harper said "The treatment of children in residential schools is a sad chapter in our history."

AN APOLOGY EXTENDED TO ALL SURVIVORS

In the fall of 1965, Elijah left the residential school and returned to the reserve to be with his family. He spent the time trapping with his father, grandfather, and uncle. Being back on the land gave him a renewed sense of pride in himself and his people. In 1967, Elijah moved to Winnipeg to finish high school. This was the first time he attended classes with white students. He adjusted well and made friends with white, Aboriginal, and Métis (people with mixed Aboriginal and European ancestry) students.

After he graduated in 1971, Elijah entered the University of Manitoba, where he studied anthropology. While at the university, Elijah married Elizabeth Ann Ross. After leaving school, Elijah took a job in Red Sucker Lake with the Manitoba Indian Brotherhood, the political organization of Manitoba's First Nations communities, where he ran a development program. In 1975, he moved back to Winnipeg to work with the Manitoba Department of Northern Affairs as a program analyst. Elijah was responsible for a huge area in Northern Manitoba, where he looked after the communities' budgets and infrastructure, such as building roads and bridges.

In March 1978, Elijah heard that there was to be an election on the Red Sucker Lake Reserve. He returned home to run for the position of chief. He wanted to work with the Indian Brotherhood, to research the idea of independence and self-sufficiency for Aboriginal people. At the time, each Aboriginal band had its own administration that was, in turn, governed by the Canadian government. Elijah believed that his people were capable of ruling themselves and wanted to work with the Brotherhood to make that happen. Elijah won the election. He was 29 years old.

When Elijah won a seat for the New Democratic Party (NDP), he became the first Treaty Indian to be elected to Parliament.

The next step for Elijah was to enter provincial politics. He believed that as a member of the Manitoba Legislative Assembly he could help bring about the changes he wanted for his people. He ran for the New Democratic Party in the riding of Rupertsland and won. On February 4, 1986, Howard Pawley, the premier of Manitoba, appointed him minister of Northern Affairs and minister in charge of the Communities Economic Development Fund Act for businesses and Crown Corporations, such as logging firms.

## Meech Lake Accord

*In 1982, the British Parliament had passed the Canada Act, which gave Canada full political independence from Britain. This was due to the work of Prime Minister Pierre Trudeau, who had fought to repatriate or "bring home" Canada's constitution. Every province, except Quebec, signed the constitution. Although Quebec was bound by the constitution's terms, it refused to sign until the constitution was changed so that it recognized Quebec as a distinct society with special privileges, within Canada.*

*In 1984, Brian Mulroney became prime minister. Mulroney pledged to get Quebec to sign the constitution. In 1987, he organized a meeting of all ten provincial premiers. There they wrote the Meech Lake Accord (named for the place where the conference was held), which recognized Quebec as a "distinct society" with special privileges. The provinces were given three years to ratify, or approve, the accord.*

Debates were held throughout the country in response to the Meech Lake Accord. Many groups did not like the accord, and Aboriginal people, in particular, felt that their collective rights were being ignored. Elijah and other Aboriginal leaders objected that Quebec and English Canada were credited as the two founding nations of the country while the First Nations were ignored. Although government leaders promised to deal with their concerns once the accord was signed, Elijah and other leaders did not believe them. After all, they said, their concerns had been ignored for over 400 years. By blocking Meech Lake, they believed they would show the rest of the country that they could, indeed, form a strong united front and wield political power on the federal level.

The deadline for ratification was Saturday June 23, 1990. Eight provinces, including Quebec, had signed. Newfoundland and Manitoba had not. The Manitoba Legislature was scheduled to vote on the Friday, which was the last day before the deadline. In order for the accord to be approved, every member of the Manitoba legislature had to vote "yes." Elijah, with the approval of his own tribal leaders, was determined to defeat the accord. The way to do this, he decided, was to hold up the vote until the deadline had passed. Elijah did this by continually raising questions and getting people to speak to them until time ran out.

At the same time, the Newfoundland government was also debating the accord. On June 22, Clyde Wells, the Newfoundland premier, called Elijah and asked what he was planning to do. Once Wells learned that Elijah was going to hold up the vote, he knew that the accord would be defeated, so Newfoundland did not vote. Manitoba, through Elijah Harper, had killed the Meech Lake Accord.

Elijah's action was controversial, but he defended it by saying that he had his people's interests at heart. He had accomplished what he set out to do—focus the nation's attention on the needs of Aboriginal Canadians.

Elijah resigned from the Manitoba legislature on November 30, 1992. In 1993, he ran for Federal office, when he joined the Liberal party and was elected to the Canadian House of Commons as a Member of Parliament (MP). In Parliament, he served on the Committee of Aboriginal Affairs and was appointed Commissioner of the Indian Claims Commission on January 21, 1999.

Over the years, Elijah has been recognized for his service and achievements. In 1991, Elijah received the Stanley Knowles Humanitarian Award. The award is presented annually by the Ontario Public Service Employees Union, to the person who best exemplifies the spirit and ideals of Stanley Knowles, a social justice advocate and parliamentarian from Winnipeg. In 1996, Elijah was given a National Aboriginal Achievement Award.

Today, Elijah Harper continues to speak out for his people by standing up to what he believes is an unfair system. Aboriginal people, he believes, have for too long, been treated as second-class citizens without the rights and privileges afforded to other Canadians. Elijah has devoted his life to changing that situation.

# Craig Kielburger

## Free the Children

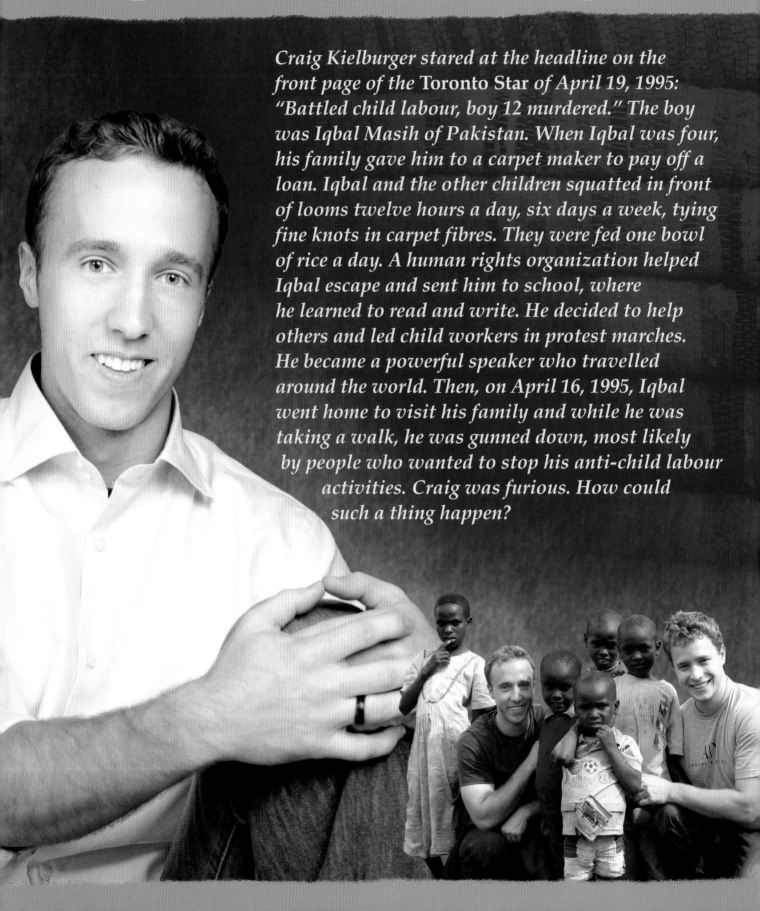

Craig Kielburger stared at the headline on the front page of the **Toronto Star** of April 19, 1995: "Battled child labour, boy 12 murdered." The boy was Iqbal Masih of Pakistan. When Iqbal was four, his family gave him to a carpet maker to pay off a loan. Iqbal and the other children squatted in front of looms twelve hours a day, six days a week, tying fine knots in carpet fibres. They were fed one bowl of rice a day. A human rights organization helped Iqbal escape and sent him to school, where he learned to read and write. He decided to help others and led child workers in protest marches. He became a powerful speaker who travelled around the world. Then, on April 16, 1995, Iqbal went home to visit his family and while he was taking a walk, he was gunned down, most likely by people who wanted to stop his anti-child labour activities. Craig was furious. How could such a thing happen?

Craig Kielburger was a typical seventh-grade student when he read Iqbal Masih's story. He asked his mother, a teacher, to help him find information on child labour. She sent him to the library where a helpful librarian showed him how to search out magazine and newspaper articles.

Craig learned that children in many countries spend their lives working in dimly lit, poorly ventilated rooms or in underground pits. They are exploited for their work, beaten, and starved. Craig wanted to help. He called human rights organizations, but the people he spoke to did not know much about child labour and did not seem to know where he could get any further information, or how he could help. Then he read about an organization called Youth Action Network (YAN) that is dedicated to helping youth become more informed and actively involved with social issues. YAN was having a fair the following Saturday. Craig and his friends thought this would be the perfect place to put up an exhibit. They decided to find out more about the event.

When Craig learned of the children around
the world forced into terrible working conditions,
he decided to take action.

Craig was only 12 years old when he became involved in the plight of children around the world, but he believed in the cause, and never let his age stand in the way.

Craig phoned YAN and spoke to Alam Rahman. Alam's parents were from Bangladesh, where there is also much child labour. Alam warmly encouraged Craig to participate in the fair, and the next day Craig asked his grade seven class for volunteers to help him put together an exhibit about child labour. Eighteen students raised their hands. That evening the group met at the Kielburger house to plan a display. One of Craig's newspaper clippings showed 250 children marching and chanting "Free the Children!" They decided to name their group Free the Children (FTC).

# From Anger to Action

*In the book* **Free the Children** *that Craig wrote with author Kevin Major, he talks about his experience:* "People sometimes ask me how I am able, as a teenager, to deal with all of the horrific things I have seen. They do affect me. At times I find myself frustrated and angry. At other times, my hatred for what I have seen can turn to despair. But I have come to realize that none of these emotions really accomplish anything. . . . My anger must move me to action; my sadness, to a determination to help."

At the fair, many people came to see the FTC exhibit. Adults thought it was wonderful that these children were so anxious to help other children halfway around the world. Their success at the fair encouraged Craig and his friends to do more. The Kielbergers' den became the FTC office. Members contacted organizations around the world. They gathered brochures and pamphlets and plastered the walls with posters. They made up information kits for schools. Craig wrote a letter about Free the Children that his principal distributed to all the schools in their district.

The group's first presentation was to a nearby school where they told stories about Iqbal and other children like him. The presentation was a success, and they repeated it at schools all around Toronto. That fall, Craig spoke to an audience of 2,000 delegates at the Ontario Federation of Labour (OFL). He told them about Iqbal and the abuses practiced against children. When the young teenager finished speaking, the applause was deafening. The OFL donated $5,000 to FTC. People in the audience donated money as well and, in all, FTC received $150,000 in pledges that day. The money was put into a special bank account for projects, such as education, that FTC could use to help working children in the developing world.

Craig's ability to involve people in his cause and spread his message of hope has made a remarkable impact around the world.

One day, Craig met Alam Rahman, whom he hadn't seen since the YAN Fair. Alam was so impressed with Craig's efforts that he invited him to come along on a visit to Bangladesh. Craig's parents did not want him to go. After all, he was not even allowed to travel downtown by himself, so how could he fly to Asia with only 24-year-old Alam to supervise him? Once Craig convinced his parents that he would be safe, he wrote to UNICEF in New York and contacted human rights organizations all over South Asia, asking them to set up meetings for him when he was there.

In Bangladesh, Craig met children who worked at the docks, loading and unloading back-breakingly heavy shipments from boats. He learned that many girls there do not go to school and are routinely hired out by their families as domestic servants. Craig and Alam then went to India, Nepal, and Pakistan, where they saw more children working in the most hopeless and unsafe conditions.

Craig's experiences deepened his desire to help exploited children. When he returned to Canada, he worked hard to build up Free the Children. He spoke at schools and to civic groups. He was interviewed by reporters and appeared on television. News about the plight of child labourers was spreading. Groups launched letter-writing campaigns and worked with the media to inform the public about abuses against kids. In Brazil, members of FTC met with the president of the country, and convinced the government to give $1 million towards programs to help child labourers. In Canada and the U.S., FTC started the Rugmark campaign, which uses a seal to tell buyers that a carpet was made without child labour. And thanks to FTC, every Reebok soccer ball now carries a "Child-Free Labor" stamp.

Through Craig's efforts and those of his friends, Free the Children has become the world's largest organization of children helping children. It has offices in Toronto, Canada, and Connecticut, U.S.A. It has built over 500 schools around the world and involved over one million children in 45 countries.

## Free the Children's Creed

*Free the Children is committed to freeing young people from the idea that they are powerless to make a difference by equipping them with the knowledge and leadership skills to be effective social advocates. Free the Children believes that young people have a right and a responsibility to participate in matters that affect them, as stated in Article 12 of the Convention on the Rights of the Child. As such, the organization provides young people with a voice by empowering them with the tools, support and guidance necessary to effect positive social change. The organization has received the World's Children's Prize for the Rights of the Child (also known as the Children's Nobel Prize), the Human Rights Award from the World Association of Non-Governmental Organizations, and has formed successful partnerships with leading school boards and Oprah's Angel Network.*

# Angel Network

*Oprah Winfrey was so impressed by Craig and the work of Free the Children that she teamed up with him to build new schools for children in countries around the world. Together they have built 59 schools in 12 countries including China, Kenya, and Sierra Leone, plus a vocational training centre in Sri Lanka.*

Craig and Free the Children have received many awards for their work. These include the Roosevelt Freedom Medal and the State of the World Forum Award. Craig has been appointed Ambassador of the Children's Embassy in Sarajevo and has been named a Global Leader of Tomorrow at the 1998 World Economic Forum in Davos, Switzerland. In October 1998, he received the Canadian Governor General's Award for Meritorious Service.

Craig believes that children all over the world need to learn that they have power and can get things done. "If children are to be free," he says, "they need to be taught to care, to dream and, most of all… to hope."

Giving children power to change their lives through education is a key point of FTC.

"...*to care, to dream and, most of all...to hope*"

~Craig Kielburger

# Hannah Taylor

## The Ladybug Foundation

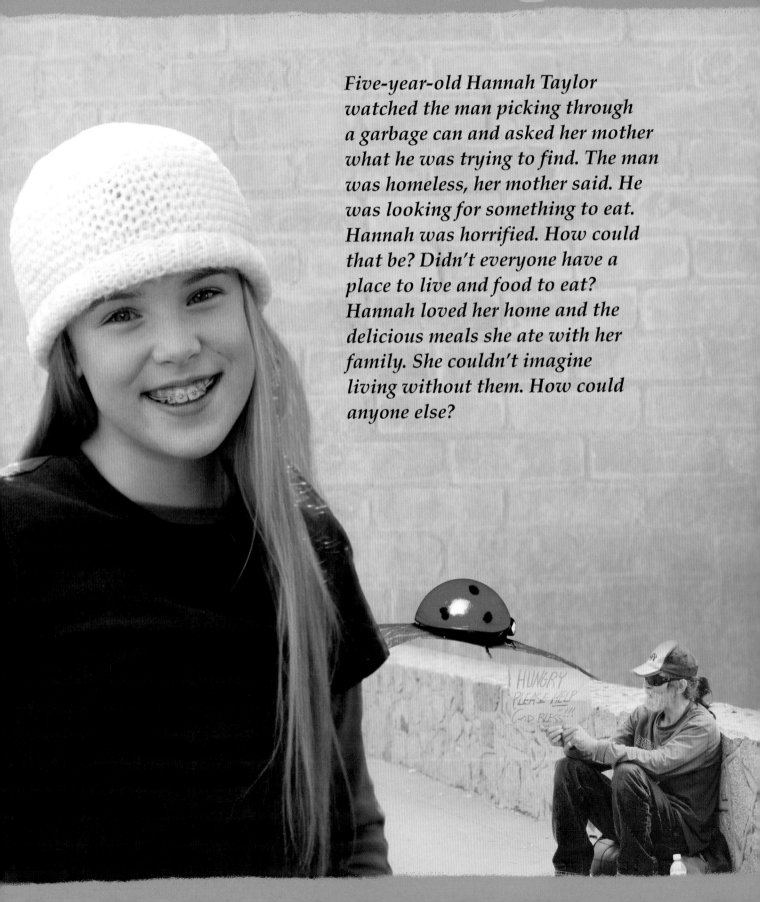

*Five-year-old Hannah Taylor watched the man picking through a garbage can and asked her mother what he was trying to find. The man was homeless, her mother said. He was looking for something to eat. Hannah was horrified. How could that be? Didn't everyone have a place to live and food to eat? Hannah loved her home and the delicious meals she ate with her family. She couldn't imagine living without them. How could anyone else?*

Hannah Taylor wanted everyone in the world to be as happy as she was. She had loving parents, a warm house, food, and plenty of toys. Yet she worried about others who didn't have what she had. Hannah felt a deep sadness when she saw people who were sleeping on the streets or begging for money. If everyone would just share a little of what they had, she thought, no one would have to go hungry.

Although she was only five years old, Hannah wanted to do something to help. She thought about the problem for a whole year. She kept asking her parents about homeless people until her mother told her that when something upsets you, you should try to find a solution. That way, she said, your heart would not feel so sad.

The next day Hannah went to her Grade One teacher and asked if she could talk to the class about homelessness and what they, as children, could do to help. Her teacher agreed and, after Hannah spoke, the children organized a bake sale. They gave the money they raised to a local mission, an organization that provides food and shelter for the homeless. That was the start of what became the Ladybug Foundation, an organization that helps the homeless.

Hannah followed her mother's advice and saw that taking action could start to effect change, even in small ways.

# Homelessness

*Homelessness is a world problem. The United Nations'
(UN) Universal Declaration of Human Rights says that
having a home is a basic human right. To study the problem,
the UN declared 1987 the International Year of Shelter for the
Homeless. According to their definition, a "homeless"
person is not only someone who lives on the street or in a
shelter, but can also be someone without protection against
bad weather, personal security, sanitary facilities, safe
drinking water, education, work, and health services. The
UN states that the right to a home must be seen as a basic
humanitarian principle, as recognized in the Universal
Declaration of Human Rights.*

*Researchers discovered that people can become homeless
for many reasons. Sometimes they lose their jobs and can't
afford to pay for housing. Mental illness or the abuse of
substances, such as drugs or alcohol, can keep a person
from working. Natural disasters, such as tornadoes or
earthquakes, can destroy people's homes.*

*Many organizations help the homeless. Communities
provide shelters where they can get food and a place to sleep.
Organizations such as Goodwill Industries offer training
courses to help people develop skills and find jobs. Still,
homelessness remains a major problem in most parts
of the world.*

Hannah had seen cans set out in stores to collect money for charities and thought she could do the same thing for the homeless. She didn't have any cans but, thanks to her baby sister, she did have a lot of baby food jars. With her mother's help, she gathered the jars and decorated them with paintings of ladybugs. She chose the ladybug design because "ladybugs are good luck and we need good luck helping homeless people. And homeless people also need good luck in their lives." Hannah called them her "Make Change" jars. She and her friends gave them to businesses, schools, and people in the community. They distributed the proceeds to missions and other organizations that, in turn, used the money to help the homeless.

Hannah chose ladybugs as a symbol of good luck.

Hannah's fundraising effort started with ladybug jars. From there, she decided that if she wanted to raise more money, she had to talk to the people she called the "Big Bosses" in downtown Winnipeg, the executives who ran companies. At first she took them to lunch, one at a time. Then she decided that if one Big Boss could help, a lot of them working together would make a huge difference. That idea became a series of "Big Bosses lunches." At the first one, Hannah drew 50 pictures and sold them. She was astounded when two men bid against each other, and her picture of a ladybug sold for $10,000!

In the first five years after she started the Ladybug Foundation, Hannah and her friends raised over $1,000,000 for the homeless. "Donations of food, clothing, and money are good ways to help the homeless," Hannah said, "but mostly what you can do is be nice to them. If they're cold, share your mitts. If they're sad, say hi to them.... If they're hungry, [give] them a sandwich. And just love them like family. They need that most of all."

Hannah has taken her own message to heart. She has made friends with people at the homeless shelters she visits. One of them, a man named Rick, cried when Hannah met him. She asked him why he was crying, and he said it was because she was being nice to him.

Hannah spends much of her time speaking at schools and businesses in Winnipeg and across Canada. She says she gets homesick when she travels, because only one of her parents can come with her each time. When she grows up, she says, she wants to be a dog breeder, an oceanographer, an archaeologist, or the Prime Minister of Canada. And, no matter what she does, Hannah, who has already published a book called *Ruby's Hope*, wants to be an author as well.

Hannah inspires other kids by telling them to follow their heart, just as she has done.

Hannah has a message for other young people who want to make a difference. She tells them: "Just follow your heart. Tell your parents about what you're doing and what you want to do and they might give you some ideas. But, really, just follow your heart, and maybe get your schoolmates involved so they can help out, too."

Hannah has accumulated many honours. She is proud to be a juror for the World's Children's Prize for the Rights of the Child: "I am the youngest member of the jury panel of children from around the world that selects the annual recipient of the World's Children's Prize for the Rights of the Child in Stockholm—sort of like a Nobel Prize for people in the world helping children. I get to do this for seven years! Nelson Mandela is a patron of this organization!" She has won other awards, including a Canada's Most Powerful Women: Future Leader award. She has had an emergency shelter named for her, and there is a National Film Board film about her. In 2007, Hannah won a BR!CK Award in the category of Community Building. This award, sponsored by corporations, is given to people under the age of 25 who improve conditions within their community. Hannah was one of twelve winners chosen from 1,000 nominees.

Hannah has a busy schedule of speaking and travelling to spread her message about tackling the problem of homelessness.

# The BR!CK Award

The BR!CK Awards were started in 1996 to honour young people who identify problems and work to solve them. When Hannah won, 1,000 people applied for the award and the judges chose 24 finalists. Much of the judging was done by the BR!CK Academy, which is a group of 72 past award winners. They were looking for young people who did something to make the world a better place. Their standards were:

1.   Has this finalist helped a lot of people?
2.   Will the effort that the finalist started get bigger and help even more people?
3.   Is this person the top young leader in his or her field?

Each finalist was interviewed three times. Then the judges met and evaluated what these people had done and how effective their efforts had been. After a few days of discussion, they chose 12 winners. BR!CK Winners who are 18 and under receive a $5,000 scholarship and a $5,000 community grant, which is paid to the winner's chosen non-profit organization. Those who are 19 to 25 receive their entire award as a community grant. And the winner of the Golden BR!CK, which is the top award, gets $100,000 in community grants.

Hannah is proud of her work and proud of the people, such as Rick, that she has met. "I have a picture of us together," said Hannah. "He wore his best shirt the day they took our picture. He is just like you and me—he just needs someone to care about him. I told him I care about him and I always will." Since then, Rick has changed his life. He now has a job and a place to live.

*"Just follow your heart."*

~Hannah Taylor

Hannah and her friend Rick.

# Canadian History Timeline

**1497**  John Cabot claims Newfoundland for Britain and charts the Gulf of St. Lawrence.

**1535**  Jacques Cartier sails to what becomes New France (Québec). He finds Iroquoians living on the island of Montréal.

**1541**  Cartier and Sieur de Roberval found the first French settlement in North America.

**1600**  King Henry IV of France grants fur trading rights in the Gulf of St. Lawrence to a group of French merchants. This begins the fur trade in Canada.

**1608**  Samuel de Champlain founds the colony of Québec.

**1638**  Henry Hudson explores the area around what is now Hudson's Bay.

**1625**  French Jesuits arrive in Québec.

**1629**  David Kirke captures Québec for Britain.

**1642**  **Jeanne Mance and Paul Chomedey de Maisonneuve found the village of Montréal.**

**1663**  Québec becomes a royal province.

**1670**  The Hudson's Bay company is formed.

**1713**  The British get possession of Hudson's Bay, Newfoundland, and Acadia (Nova Scotia); Cape Breton remains in French hands.

**1749**  Britain founds the city of Halifax.

**1752**  Canada's first newspaper, the *Halifax Gazette*, is launched.

**1754**  France and Britain fight over territory in the French and Indian War.

**1755**  Britain expels the Acadians from Nova Scotia. Many go to New Orleans and become today's Cajuns.

**1759**  General Wolfe defeats Montcalm on the Plains of Abraham.

**1763**  The Treaty of Paris gives French territory in Canada to Britain. The treaty sets aside land for Aboriginal people, stating that the government has the exclusive right to negotiate treaties.

**1774**  *The Québec Act* assures religious freedom for Roman Catholics. Québec will have French civil law and British criminal law.

**1783**  Following the American Revolution, the border between Canada and the United States is established. It extends from the Atlantic Ocean to the Lake of the Woods on the border of Ontario and Manitoba in Canada and Minnesota in the U.S.

**1791**  *The Constitutional Act* divides Canada into Lower Canada (now Québec) and Upper Canada (now Ontario).

**1792**  George Vancouver explores Canada's Pacific coast.

**1812**  The War of 1812 breaks out, pitting Canada and Britain against the United States. The war ends in 1814 with the Treaty of Ghent.

**1818**  The 49th parallel is designated as the official border between Canada and the United States from Lake of the Woods west to the Rocky Mountains.

**1836**  Canada's first railway, the Champlain and Saint Lawrence Railroad, opens.

**1841**  *The Act of Union* unites Lower and Upper Canada.

**1849**  Canada begins an official policy of bilingualism. The U.S./Canadian border is extended to the Pacific Ocean.

**1851**  **Slaves use the Underground Railway network to escape from the U.S. to Canada.**

**1857**  Ottawa is named Canada's official capital.

**1860**  The Civil War breaks out in the United States.

**1865**  Charlottetown and Québec conferences set up a structure for Canadian confederation. The Civil War ends.

**1867**  Canada becomes a confederation known as the Dominion of Canada. Sir John A. Macdonald becomes the country's first prime minister. The provinces are Ontario, Quebec, Nova Scotia, and New Brunswick.